Beginners' Polish

Joanna Michalak-Gray

Advisory editor
Susan Johnson

Revised by
Agnieszka Murdoch

First published in Great Britain in 2009 by Hodder and Stoughton. An Hachette UK company.
Previously published in 2013 as *Get Started in Polish.*

This updated edition published by Teach Yourself in 2025
An imprint of John Murray Press

2

Editorial support from Haremi Ltd

A CIP catalogue record for this title is available from the British Library

Paperback ISBN 978 1 39982 1 988
ebook ISBN 978 1 39982 1 995

Typeset by Integra Software Services Pvt. Ltd., Pondicherry, India

Printed and bound in Great Britain by Clays Ltd, Elcograf S.p.A.

John Murray Press policy is to use papers that are natural, renewable and recyclable products and made from wood grown in sustainable forests. The logging and manufacturing processes are expected to conform to the environmental regulations of the country of origin.

John Murray Press
Carmelite House
50 Victoria Embankment
London EC4Y 0DZ

www.teachyourself.com

John Murray Press, part of Hodder & Stoughton Limited
An Hachette UK company

The authorised representative in the EEA is Hachette Ireland,
8 Castlecourt Centre, Dublin 15, D15 XTP3, Ireland (email: info@hbgi.ie)

Contents

Acknowledgements v

About the course vi

Learn to learn viii

Useful expressions xiv

Pronunciation guide xvi

1 **Jestem Andrew** *I'm Andrew*
Introduce yourself • State your nationality and profession • Address somebody politely • Invite somebody in • Say you are hungry or tired 2

2 **To jest mój pies, Azor** *This is my dog, Azor*
Introduce others • Talk about family • Ask and answer questions about personal details • Describe people and animals 12

3 **Jestem szczęśliwy – mam czas i pieniądze** *I'm happy – I've got time and money*
Say you have or haven't got something • Ask and answer questions about relationships • Talk about things you have • Talk about things you do 22

Review 1 32

4 **Muszę już iść** *I've got to go now*
Tell the time and handle numbers • Describe your plans • Describe what you must/have to do or don't have to do • Agree to meet someone 34

5 **Chciał(a)bym zamówić stolik** *I'd like to book a table*
Ask how someone is • Ask for help and information • Say numbers 0–100 • Say you would or wouldn't like to do something 44

6 **Poproszę lody** *Can I have an ice cream, please?*
Ask for things politely • Order food • Ask for and pay the check • Buy stamps and postcards 54

Review 2 64

7 **Lubię kuchnię polską** *I like Polish cuisine*
Express likes and dislikes • Express preferences • Talk about food and cuisines • Find simple information in menus 68

8 **Czy można zapłacić kartą?** *Can I pay by card?*
Ask for permission • Say what needs to be done • Say what is and is not allowed • Say what is worth doing • Understand and give simple directions 78

9 **Wszystkiego najlepszego z okazji urodzin** *Happy birthday*
Ask questions • Indicate time • Arrange a meeting • Describe a location • Indicate frequency 88

10 **Jak dojechać do . . . ?** *How do we get to . . . ?*
Give and understand street directions • Describe distances • Use compass directions such as *east* and *west* 98

Review 3 108

Answer key 112

Polish–English glossary 130

Grammar appendix 136

Conversation translations 145

Can-do statements 152

Acknowledgements

I would like to thank my family, especially Ian for his patience, support and encouragement, and friends too numerous to mention individually by name in England and Poland for their direct and indirect contributions. A special thanks to Nigel Gotteri for his considerable contribution to this course and to Chris and Isla Adamek, Anna and Rob Marfleet, Helena McDougall and Brenda Rabbidge, for being enthusiastic students and patient recipients of all good and not so good ideas which shaped this course. As always I owe a great debt of gratitude to the editors, particularly Alexandra Jaton, Helen Vick, Helen Hart and the reviewers.

For the 2nd edition my heartfelt thanks go to Sarah Cole, Helen Hart, Susan Johnson and Rebecca Moeller for their guidance, encouragement and support.

Any flak should, of course, be directed straight at the author.

About the course

Learning a foreign language is always exciting, but learning on your own can be daunting. *Beginners' Polish* will make the task of learning Polish alone a lot less daunting. Each unit in the book is centered on a single topic and includes three or more conversations. You can listen to the conversations, practice your pronunciation and speaking, practice reading and writing in Polish, all on a single subject which will reinforce and encourage your comprehension.

Here are the main features of each teaching unit:

Culture points introduce various aspects of life in Poland and show new Polish words in a context that is easy to understand.

Vocabulary builder presents new words grouped by theme related to the unit topic. A list of new expressions presents additional vocabulary that you will need to understand the conversations in the unit. Some words in brackets will appear in pairs separated by the symbol >. These will always be verbs. This course systematically puts the imperfective verb first with the arrowhead pointing towards the perfective. Although the system is used right from the start you will find a full explanation in Unit 10.

Conversations follow a story with characters you will meet throughout the course. Don't be afraid to learn the dialogues by heart. Copy the conversations and display them (walls, fridge doors, kitchen cupboards). You can mix the pieces up and put the conversations together again. Translate each conversation into English and display the pieces with just one side of the conversation and try to complete it by saying out loud the other side – the possibilities are endless.

Listen to the conversations several times. You will soon begin to hear when one word ends and another begins. After a few more times you will be able to understand everything that is said. And finally, you will feel confident enough to repeat whole sentences.

Language discovery presents activities that will help you put the language together for yourself and explains how the Polish in each unit is put together. You will find varying types of facts and information related to the unit's language points. **Practice** exercises are included, and a **Pronunciation** section will guide you step by step.

Listen and understand offers additional listening practice with activities.

Go further presents a variety of information related to the unit topic.

Test yourself contains exercises. These can be turned into flash cards and used to create your own language quiz. Just write the correct answers on the back of the card in pencil (so it's not very visible). Collect the cards and spend five, ten or 15 minutes going over them every day while waiting for the bus, or train. Successful learning depends on repetition and revision and the cards help.

You will also find **Review units**, an **Answer key**, a **Polish–English glossary**, and a **Grammar appendix**.

The course is accompanied by audio for the conversations, some exercises, and parts of the self-test at the end of each unit.

Try to practice each skill every day.

The icons in the progress tracker are used throughout the book to help you easily identify and locate the skills you want to practice:

 Listening skills

 Speaking – pronunciation skills

 Reading skills

 Writing skills

 Speaking – conversation skills

Remember: there are many ways to build your skills in addition to those provided in this book: use a language-learning app, listen to music or podcasts, watch TV shows or movies, go to a restaurant, follow social media accounts in Polish, read blogs, newspapers or magazines, switch the language settings in your apps to Polish, or sign up for a language exchange or a tutor.

Learn to learn

The Discovery method

There are lots of approaches to language learning, some practical and some quite unconventional. Perhaps you know a few, or even have techniques of your own. In this book we have incorporated the **Discovery method** of learning, a sort of DIY approach to language learning. What this means is that you will be encouraged throughout the course to engage your mind and figure out the language for yourself, through identifying patterns, understanding grammar concepts, noticing words that are similar to English, and more.

Simply put, if you **figure something out for yourself**, you're more likely to understand it. And when you use what you've learned, you're more likely to remember it. And because many of the essential but (let's admit it!) daunting details, such as grammar rules, are taught through the **Discovery method**, you'll have more fun while learning. Soon, the language will start to make sense and you'll be relying on your own intuition to construct original sentences *independently*, not just listening and repeating.

Everyone can succeed in learning a language—the key is to know *how to learn it*.

How to be a successful language learner

There are many strategies that can help you become a successful language learner. Different people have different learning styles and some of these approaches will be more effective for you than others. Use this list as a point of inspiration when you want to find the most effective ways to advance your skills and begin your journey to fluency.

VOCABULARY

Words are the building blocks of language. The more you use the words you're introduced to, the more quickly they'll lodge into your memory. These study tips will help you remember better:

- Organize your study of vocabulary. Group new words under **generic categories**, e.g. *food*, *furniture*; **situations** in which they occur, e.g. under *restaurant* you can write *server*, *table*, *menu*, *check* and **functions**, e.g. greetings, parting, thanks, apologizing.
- Say the words out loud as you read them.
- Write new words over and over. List them on your phone or tablet, and remember: you can usually switch the keyboard to include accents and special characters.
- Listen to the audio several times and say the words out loud as you hear or read them.
- Cover up the English translations and try to remember the meanings.
- Associate the words with similar-sounding words in English, e.g. **recepcja** ~ *reception*.
- Create flash cards, drawings and mind maps.
- Write Polish words for objects around your house and stick them to objects.
- Pay attention to patterns in words, e.g. adding **dobry** to **dzień** (*day*), **wieczór** (*evening*) or **noc** (*night*), creates a greeting or farewell – **dzień dobry**, **dobry wieczór** or **dobranoc**.
- **Experiment with words.** Use the words that you learn in new contexts and find out if they are correct. For example, you learn in Unit 5 that **godzina** means *hour* in the context of time, e.g., in **która godzina**? Experiment with **godzina** in new contexts, e.g., **za godzinę**, **na którą godzinę?**, **na czarną godzinę** . . . Check the new phrases either in this book, a dictionary or with Polish speakers.

GRAMMAR

Grammar gives your language structure. It allows you to experiment with the vocabulary you learn because you'll understand how they work together to create meaning. In other words, you'll begin to develop a feel for the language. Here are some tips to help you study more effectively:

- Check the **Grammar appendix** for terms you don't understand.
- **Experiment with grammar rules.** Compare the rules for Polish to those of other languages you know. Predict rules, and be ready to spot exceptions. You'll remember them better and get a feel for the language.
- Write your own glossary. Keep a 'pattern bank' that organizes examples by structure.
- Use vocabulary to practice new structures. When you learn a new verb form, write the conjugation of verbs that follow the same form.

PRONUNCIATION

The best way to improve your pronunciation is simply to practice as much as possible. Study individual sounds first, then full words and sentences. Don't forget, it's not just about pronouncing letters and words correctly, but using the right intonation. So, when practicing words and sentences, mimic the intonation of the Polish speakers you hear.

- Study individual sounds, then full words. Make a list of problem words and practice them. Always be aware of intonation; mimic the rising and falling sounds you hear.
- Repeat the conversations, line by line. Listen to yourself and try to mimic what you hear. Record yourself if you can.
- Keep a section of your notebook for pronunciation rules and practise those that trouble you.

LISTENING AND READING

The conversations and listening and reading activities in this book include questions to help guide you in your understanding. But you can go further by following some of these tips.

- **Imagine the situation.** Try to imagine the scenes, and make educated guesses about the topic and vocabulary – a conversation in a café is likely to be about drinks or food.
- **Get the gist.** Concentrate on the main parts to get the gist and don't worry about individual words.

- **Guess the meaning of words.** Use your own experience or knowledge of the topic to guess the sorts of words in a reading or dialogue, and use context – the sense of nearby words, sentences, or paragraphs – to guess the meaning of specific words in the passage.

WRITING

You'll have plenty of writing practice using this book. Creating vocabulary lists, grammar summaries and taking good notes as you study is another great opportunity to practice writing. If you're keeping your lists or notes on your phone, computer or tablet, remember to switch the keyboard language to be able to include all accents and special characters. Here are some other ways to practice writing:

- Write out the answers to all Practice and Test Yourself questions.
- Create your own vocabulary lists and a grammar summary.
- Look up writing prompts for language learning or try writing a daily gratitude journal in Polish.
- Write out your To Do and shopping lists in Polish.
- Join online forums and discussion groups about or in Polish.

SPEAKING

The greatest obstacle to speaking a new language is the fear of making a mistake. Keep in mind that you make mistakes in your own language—it's simply part of the human condition. Accept it. Most errors are not serious and they will not affect the meaning, so concentrate on getting your message across and use the mistakes as learning opportunities.

Here are some useful tips to help you practice speaking Polish:

- Speak out as you go through the course. Answer questions out loud. Rehearse dialogues out loud, then try to replace sentences with ones that are true for you. Remember to mimic the speakers' pronunciation.
- Translate the world around you. Look at objects and try to name them in Polish. Look at people and try to describe them in detail. After you have conducted a sales transaction in your own language, do it in Polish. That is, buy the gift or order the food, in Polish!
- Keep talking. The best way to improve your fluency is to talk every time you have the opportunity to do so: keep the conversations flowing and don't worry about the mistakes. If you get stuck on a particular word, don't let the conversation stop – simplify what you want to say, paraphrase or replace the unknown word with one you do know.

- Realize that many errors are not serious. Some types of errors do not affect meaning, as in using the wrong ending (**kawa** instead of **kawę**), wrong gender (**dentysta** instead of **dentystka**) or wrong adjective ending (**zajęty** instead of **zajęta**).

Before you start

A little goes a long way!

Try to use the book little and often, rather than for long stretches at a time. This will help you to create a study habit, much in the same way you would learn a sport or music. Leave the book somewhere handy so that you can pick it up for just a few minutes to refresh your memory.

Before you start, make a plan!

Setting goals affects the programming of your brain, strengthening neural pathways and ultimately making it more likely that you will achieve those goals. Before you begin, think about how much time you want to devote to learning, which skills or areas you want to focus on, and identify specific ideas you want to be able to communicate or activities you want to engage in.

Track your progress!

Start a notebook to use for study, where you can create vocabulary lists, a grammar summary, questions you'd like answered, etc. Keep track of your resources—write down the names of films, podcasts, songs or blogs you like, and jot down a few words or expressions you may have recognized or learned. The more you can reflect on your learning process, the deeper your connection with the language will be. If you need more guidance in this process, we recommend Teach Yourself *Fluentish: Language Learning Planner & Journal* by Jo Franco.

Use the tools at the beginning of each unit to help you set goals, plan your time, and keep track of the work you do.

IN THIS UNIT, YOU WILL LEARN HOW TO

Each unit begins with an overview of the language you will be learning and skills you will be acquiring.

MY PROGRESS TRACKER

Use the progress tracker to plan your study time and to keep a record of what you've accomplished. The first column tracks time, and the remaining five columns represent the skills you'll be working on: listening, pronunciation, reading, writing, and spoken interaction.

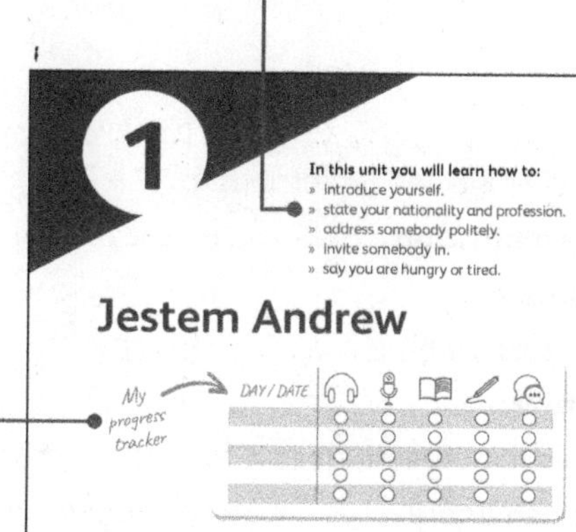

Personalize the tracker: Instead of the date or day, you can enter an increment of time (15 minutes, 1 hour...). Add columns for culture, vocabulary, grammar or any other area you wish to focus on. Give yourself a star when you feel you've done particularly well. Make it your own! Review your tracker regularly and see which areas could use more practice.

Use the **Self check** at the end of each unit to evaluate your progress.

Learning a language takes work. But the work can be a lot of fun. So, let's begin!

Useful expressions

00.01 An easy way to learn Polish **'please and thank you's'** is to remember the expressions as **3P + D**:

przepraszam *excuse me/I'm sorry*

proszę *please/here you are*

przykro mi *I'm sorry.*

dziękuję *thank you*

Similarly, **greetings and farewells** can be remembered as **4Ds**:

dzień dobry *good morning/afternoon*

do widzenia *goodbye*

dobry wieczór *good evening*

dobranoc *goodnight*

Proszę (*please*) can be combined with a number of other words to express a **polite request**:

Polish	Polish	English
Proszę +	**wejść.**	*Please come in.*
	wyjść.	*Please leave.*
	powtórzyć.	*Please repeat.*
	napisać.	*Please write it down.*
	mówić wolniej.	*Please speak more slowly.*
	przeliterować.	*Please spell it.*
	zaczekać.	*Please wait.*
	podpisać.	*Please sign.*
	usiąść.	*Please sit down.*
	wezwać lekarza.	*Please call a doctor.*
	wezwać policję.	*Please call the police.*
	wezwać straż pożarną.	*Please call the fire brigade.*

IF IN DOUBT . . .

Co to znaczy? *What does it mean?*
Jak to wymówić? *How do you pronounce it?*
Jak to powiedzieć po polsku? *How do you say it in Polish?*
Nie rozumiem. *I don't understand.*
Nie wiem. *I don't know.*
Nie jestem pewien/pewna. *I'm not sure* (masculine/feminine).

SHORT ANSWERS

tak *yes*
nie *no*
nie ma za co *not at all/don't mention it/you're welcome*

SIGNS WORTH KNOWING

wejście *entrance*
wyjście *exit*
toaleta (męska/damska) *toilets (gents/ladies)*
przymierzalnia *fitting room*

Things you mustn't do are expressed using the word **zakaz**:

Polish	Polish	English
Zakaz +	**wstępu**	*No entry (on foot)*
	wjazdu	*No entry (by vehicle)*
	palenia	*No smoking*
	fotografowania	*No photography*
	wyrzucania śmieci	*No rubbish*

IN AN EMERGENCY . . .

Ratunku! *Help!*
numer alarmowy *emergency phone number (112 for all three emergency services)*
pogotowie ratunkowe *ambulance (999)*
straż pożarna *fire service (998)*
policja *police (997)*
apteka *pharmacy*
szpital; przychodnia *hospital; outpatient surgery*
kościół; kaplica *church; chapel*

Pronunciation guide

00.02 Polish has a reputation for being a language with difficult grammar and even more difficult pronunciation. With many people of Polish heritage living in the UK, the US and in other countries, as well as millions of tourists and business people visiting Poland every year, a lot of people who face the need to pronounce Polish names like **Leszczyński**, **Trzebniewski**, **Grzegorzewski** or **Tchórzewski** would concur with that view. Yet things are not as they might seem. Polish words may look daunting to an English speaker's eye, but once you've learned some ground rules, you'll be delighted to discover how consistent Polish pronunciation is. In huge contrast to the situation in English, you'll immediately be able to pronounce Polish words when you see them for the first time. This includes the names of Polish people and places, however obscure; as long as you don't panic and don't rush, you'll be fine.

Polish, like English, uses the Latin alphabet. Compared to English, q, v and x are missing from normal Polish spelling, but the total number of letters in the Polish alphabet is brought up from a mere 23 (English's 26 minus 3) to 32 by extra letters with squiggles: an acute accent over, a tail under, a line through or a dot over:

ą, ć, ę, ł, ń, ó, ś, ź, ż

The letters **ą** and **ę** can be described as **a z ogonkiem** and **e z ogonkiem** (with a little tail). The final letters of the Polish alphabet are **ź** [ziet] or **zet z kreską** (zee with an accent) and **ż** [żet] or **zet z kropką** (zee with a dot). The acute accent ´ is known as **kreska** in Polish, so **ć**, etc. can be described as **z kreską** (with an accent). Remember that the **kreska** (acute accent) ´ does not indicate stress or emphasis but instead changes the letter's pronunciation.

Here is the order of the **Polish alphabet**:

a, ą, b, c, ć, d, e, ę, f, g, h, i, j, k, l, ł, m, n, ń, o, ó, p, r, s, ś, t, u, w, y, z, ź, ż

Each of the letters represents a distinct sound of its own, apart from **ó** and **u**, which represent exactly the same sound. The two letters with tails (**z ogonkiem**) can represent a succession of two sounds.

Sometimes a pair of letters represents a single sound: **ch**, **cz**, **dz**, **dż**, **rz**, **sz**.

Stress (emphasis, accent) almost always falls on the second-to-last syllable of a word. Exceptions like **Ameryka**, where the accent is put on the third syllable from the end [a-me-ry-ka], abbreviations and certain verb forms will be noted in Unit 9.

Points to bear in mind:

- Stress (emphasis on a particular part of a word) is quite light.
- Unstressed syllables are pronounced as clearly as stressed ones (a help when you're learning endings).

The most important thing to remember about Polish intonation is that statements in which your voice falls towards the end of a sentence can be turned into questions just by raising the pitch of your voice at the end.

We will develop all these points, and more, as we go along in each unit.

00.03 VOWELS

Polish has nine vowels:

a, ą, e, ę, i, o, ó, u, y

- The letter **a** represents a sound midway between the *a* in *father* and the *a* in *bat* or *map*.
- The letter **e** represents a sound like *e* in *bet* or *step*.
- The letter **i** represents a sound like long *e* in *clean*, *keen* or *knees*.
- The letter **o** is like the *o* in *box* or *pot*.
- The letters **ó** and **u** represent the same sound, e.g. the **ó** in **Bóg**, *God*, is similar to the *ou* in *you*.
- The letter **y** represents a sound like the short *i* in *bid* (but further away from the *i* in *bleed*).
- The tailed nasal letters **ą** and **ę** sound like *o* as in *box* and *e* as in *bed*, lengthened by an *m* or some other nasal sound. Sometimes this is closer to an *n*, *m*, or *ng*. Sometimes, especially before **ł** or at the end of words ending in **-ę**, the second element disappears altogether.

CONSONANTS

b, c, ć, d, f, g, h, j, k, l, ł, m, n, ń, p, r, s, ś, t, w, z, ź, ż

- One of the reasons why many words don't pose pronunciation problems is that some Polish letters are pronounced much like their English counterparts: *b, d, f, g, k, l, m, n, p, s, t, z*.
- It's worth remembering that **p, t**, and **k** should not be pronounced with the puff of air that usually follows them in English. *Poland* is **Polska**, not [P-holska]!

- The **l** sound in Polish is generally similar to the sound at the beginning of the word *little*.
- The remaining consonants are: **c, ć, g, h, j, ł, ń, r, ś, w, ż, ź**
- The letter **c** normally represents *ts* as in *cats*. Its name is [tse] (like English *outset* but without the *ou* and the final *t*), represented the Polish way as: [ce]. English ears perceive this *ts* as two sounds, but for Polish speakers it's a single sound, as in the middle of the name **Jacek** (ja-tsek). The name of the letter [ce] reflects the way the letter is pronounced unless it comes before **h, i** or **z**.
- The letter **j** normally represents the same sound as the *y* in English *yes*.
- The letter **ł** now normally represents a sound like the English *w*; most Polish speakers now pronounce it like the *w* in English *mower*. This letter does not have a strong sound, and you may well get the impression it has disappeared when someone speaking fast pronounces **chciała** as [chciaa].
- The letter **r** represents a rolled (trilled) *r*, as in Russian or Spanish.
- The letter **w** represents the same sound as an English *v*.
- Letters **ć, ń, ś, ź** are discussed in more detail in Unit 3.

VOICED AND VOICELESS CONSONANTS

Consonants can also be divided into two groups according to how they are produced: **voiced** or **voiceless**. Most of the voiced consonants have their voiceless counterparts. So which ones are which?

Voiced consonants	Voiceless consonants
b	p
d	t
g	k
w	f
z	s
ż	sz
rz*	sz
dż	cz
dź	ć

Two-letter combinations (**ch, rz, sz, cz, dz, dż** and **dź**) represent one sound and equal one consonant.

Voiced consonants vibrate the vocal chords as the sound is pronounced. Their corresponding **voiceless consonants** use the same shape of the mouth to pronounce the sound but without causing the vocal chords to vibrate.

If you place two fingers (index and middle finger) on the voice box (i.e. halfway down your neck) you can feel a vibration when you pronounce zzzzzzzzz (voiced) but not when you pronounce ssssss (voiceless).

Voiceless consonants are more powerful and influential because they can affect how voiced consonants behave. In fact, they can turn them into voiceless ones in a process known as de-voicing.

All these points will be developed throughout the course.

1

In this unit you will learn how to:

» introduce yourself.
» state your nationality and profession.
» address somebody politely.
» invite somebody in.
» say you are hungry or tired.

Jestem Andrew

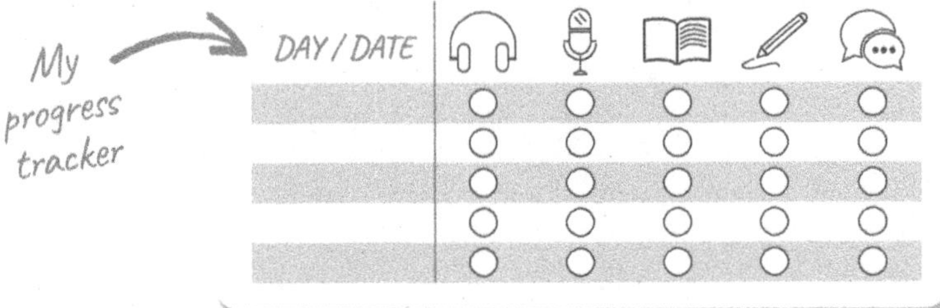

Greeting people in Polish

Greetings! When Polish speakers greet each other they may say **dzień dobry** (*good morning/afternoon*) or **dobry wieczór** (*good evening*). If they say farewell they may say **do widzenia** (*goodbye*) or **dobranoc** (*good night*). If they are in an informal situation and are well known to each other, they may greet each other by saying **cześć** (*hi/hello*), which can also be used as a farewell. When greeting close friends, they may also say **hej**, and they may use the very familiar and informal **pa** to say goodbye.

When meeting a **Polka** (*Polish woman*) or **Polak** (*Polish man*) for the first time, it's common to shake hands when introducing yourself. **Polacy** (*Polish people*) **witają** (*greet*) their family and friends with a hug or a kiss on the cheek. Older generations often give two or even three kisses. It is also common for men to shake hands whenever they say hello to people they already know, as well as when meeting someone for the first time.

Look at the words in bold above. Can you figure out what the words for *good*, *evening* and *night* are in Polish?

Vocabulary builder

01.01 **Listen as you look at the words and phrases and complete the English translations. Then listen again and try to imitate the speakers.**

GREETINGS AND SALUTATIONS

dzień dobry	*good* ______
dobry wieczór	*good* ______
dobranoc	*good* ______
do widzenia	*good* ______
pani	*Madam/Mrs/Ms; lady*
panu (pan)	*Sir/Mr,* ______
Bardzo mi miło.	______ *to meet you.*

Many Polish verbs have two versions: perfective and imperfective. Perfective verbs emphasize the completion of an action, while imperfective verbs place emphasis on the process or indicate repeated actions.

NEW EXPRESSIONS

jestem (być)	*I'm (to be)*
proszę (prosić > poprosić)	*please*
wejść	*come in/go in*
usiąść (siadać > usiąść)	*to sit down*
jest (być)	he/she/it is
zmęczony (męczyć > zmęczyć)	*tired*
tak	*yes*
trochę	*a little bit*
głodny	*hungry*
Szkotem (Szkot)	*Scot(sman)*
Anglikiem (Anglik)	*Englishman*
Brazylijką (Brazylijka)	*Brazilian (woman)*
Brazylijczykiem (Brazylijczyk)	*Brazilian (man)*
Japonką (Japonka)	*Japanese (woman)*
Japończykiem (Japończyk)	*Japanese (man)*
Nigeryjką (Nigeryjka)	*Nigerian (woman)*
Nigeryjczykiem (Nigeryjczyk)	*Nigerian (man)*
Francuzką (Francuzka)	*French (woman)*
Francuzem (Francuz)	*French (man)*
Czym się pan/pani zajmuje?	*What do you do for a living?*
emerytką (emerytka)	*retired woman*
prywatnym (prywatny)	*private*
detektywem (detektyw)	*detective*

In the vocabulary lists the basic form appears in parentheses ( ).

Answer *Yes* or *No*.

- **a** The term **wejść** means *to go out*.
- **b** **Jest** means *you are*.
- **c** *Tired* in Polish is **zmęczony**.

Conversation

01.02 *Andrew Stewart is visiting Poland to trace his family roots. He's visiting Maria Grajewska, a retired archivist he met over the internet who runs a specialist genealogy website.*

1 What word do both Andrew and Maria use to introduce themselves?

Andrew	Dzień dobry pani. Jestem Andrew Stewart.
Maria	Dzień dobry panu. Jestem Maria Grajewska.
Andrew	Bardzo mi miło.
Maria	Proszę wejść. Proszę usiąść. Czy jest pan zmęczony?
Andrew	Tak, trochę.
Maria	A czy jest pan głodny?
Andrew	Nie. Nie jestem głodny.

2 Now read the conversation and answer the questions.

- **a** What time of day is Andrew visiting Maria, daytime or evening?
- **b** What does **dzień dobry** mean?
- **c** Why does Andrew say **Bardzo mi miło**?
- **d** What does Maria mean by saying **Proszę wejść**?
- **e** **Proszę usiąść** means ________.
- **f** Andrew is not hungry so he says ________.
- **g** How would you ask a man if he is tired?
- **h** What does Andrew mean when he says **Tak, trochę**?

3 Find the expressions in the conversation that mean:

- **a** no
- **b** yes
- **c** tired
- **d** hungry

Language discovery

Look at the sentences from the conversation. Find the words in Polish for the words in parentheses.

a (*I am*) Jestem Andrew Stewart.
b (*Are you*) A czy jest pan głodny?
c (*Mrs*) Dzień dobry pani.

1 POLISH SURNAMES

Many typical Polish surnames end in **-ski** or **-cki** for men and **-ska** or **-cka** for women. Polish distinguishes masculine and feminine surnames like these by giving them different endings.

Jakub Grajewski	**Julia Grajewska**
Tomasz Forsycki	**Maria Forsycka**

2 ADDRESSING POLISH PEOPLE BY NAME

Polish people maintain three broad levels of formality in the way they address each other by name.

- The most formal of all, very official, using **pan** (*Sir*) or **pani** (*Ms/Mrs*) + surname to address people they don't know.

pan (Jakub) Grajewski/pani (Maria) Grajewska.

- Less formal, quite neutral, using **pan/pani** + first name.

pan Jakub/pani Maria

- Informal, using just the first name, often in diminutive (affectionate) form.

Antoni/Antek/Antoś

3 GENDER WORD ENDINGS

- A fundamental principle of Polish is that word endings show gender. Gender endings show how a word relates to other words in the sentence.

Jestem Irlandką. *I'm Irish (an Irishwoman).*

- Nouns are masculine, feminine or neuter. Most masculine nouns end in a consonant (a letter other than the vowels **a, e, i, o, u** or **y**), most feminine nouns end in **-a**, and most neuter nouns end in **-o** or **-e**. In Polish, people and things show gender.

Polka = nationality noun for a Polish woman

Polak = nationality noun for a Polish man

księżyc (*moon*), **statek** (*ship*) = masculine

radio (*radio*), **piwo** (*beer*) = neuter

- The ending of these words will change if you use them with a word like **Jestem** (*I'm*):

Jestem Polką.	*I'm Polish.* (woman)	**Jestem Angielką.**	*I'm English.* (woman)
Jestem Polakiem.	*I'm Polish.* (man)	**Jestem Anglikiem.**	*I'm English.* (man)

- Descriptive words (adjectives) adapt to the gender of the nouns they accompany. So if the noun is masculine, the modifying adjective is also masculine. Adjectives in their masculine form typically end in **-y**, adjectives in their feminine form end in **-a** and adjectives in their neuter form end in **-e**. The same rule applies to nationalities, which are nouns in Polish but translate into English as adjectives. You will learn more about how to talk about nationalities later in this chapter.

Jestem Anglikiem.	*I'm English.*	**Jestem zmęczony.**	*I'm tired.*

- On the other hand, if **pani** Kasia were English and tired she would say:

Jestem Angielką.	*I'm English.*	**Jestem zmęczona.**	*I'm tired.*

4 THE VERB *BYĆ (TO BE)* AND PRONOUNS

Remember the two forms of the verb **być** (*to be*): **jestem** (*I am*) and **jest** (*s/he/it is*).

Jestem already means *I am*. Include **ja** only for emphasis, as in:

Ja jestem Polką. *It's me who's Polish.*

For he/she/it, **on**, **ona** or **ono** makes the gender clear and even emphasizes which person you mean.

On jest zmęczony. *He is tired.*

5 NEGATION

Negation in Polish works simply and consistently. Most of the time you put **nie** before the verb.

Jestem zmęczony/na.	*I'm tired.*	**Nie jestem zmęczony/na.**	*I'm not tired.*

Practice

1 **Choose the correct word to complete the sentences.**
 a Ewa says: **Jestem (Polakiem/Polką).**
 b Patrick says: **Jestem (Irlandczykiem/Irlandką).**
 c Julia says: **Jestem (pracowity/pracowita).**
 d Tom says: **Jestem (zajęty/zajęta).**

2 **Answer T (true) or F (false).**
 a Include **nie** for emphasis.
 b A masculine adjective can describe a feminine noun.
 c Use **on** or **ona** to emphasize gender.
 d The endng **-ski** on a surname is feminine.

Pronunciation

01.03 Can you pronounce **W Szczebrzeszynie chrząszcz brzmi w trzcinie***? This famous tongue twister held the top spot in the *Guinness World Records* for the most difficult sentence for English speakers, but many Polish words don't look terrifying and don't cause problems for English speakers.

**In Szczebrzeszyn a beetle buzzes in the reeds.*

1 **Listen and repeat.**

problem (*problem*)	**telefon** (*phone*)	**dokument** (*document*)
kot (*cat*)	**komputer** (*computer*)	**mapa** (*map*)
lampa (*lamp*)	**mama** (*mum*)	**plan** (*plan*)
katedra (*cathedral*)	**tata** (*dad*)	**dom** (*house*)
okno (*window*)	**brat** (*brother*)	**bilet** (*ticket*)
radio (*radio*)	**numer** (*number*)	

Conversation

01.04 *Listen to Maria and Andrew get to know each other.*

1 What are the two topics of conversation?

Maria	Czy jest pan Szkotem czy Anglikiem?
Andrew	Jestem pół Szkotem i pół Anglikiem.
	A pani? Czy pani jest Polką?
Maria	Tak, jestem Polką, ale mam szkockie korzenie.
Andrew	Czym się pani zajmuje?
Maria	Jestem emerytką. A pan?
Andrew	Jestem prywatnym detektywem.
Maria	Naprawdę?

2 Now read the conversation and answer the questions.

- **a** What does Maria say to describe her nationality?
- **b** What does Maria mean when she says **mam szkockie korzenie**?
- **c** How would you ask a man if he is Scottish or English?
- **d** How does Andrew describe his profession?
- **e** How would you ask: *What do you do for a living, madam*?
- **f** What does **pół** mean?
- **g** Answer Yes or No – **ale** means *or.*

3 Match the words with their meanings.

a detektywem	**1** private
b emerytką	**2** really
c prywatnym	**3** retired
d naprawdę	**4** detective

Language discovery

1 01.05 **Listen to the audio and repeat. Fill in the blanks.**

1 SINGULAR

Polish		English	Example
ja (m/f)	**jestem**	*I am*	**Jestem zmęczony/ zmęczona.** (*I am tired.*)
ty (m/f)	**jesteś**	*you are*	**Jesteś zmęczony/ zmęczona.** (*You are tired.*)
on (m)	**jest**	*he is*	**On jest** ________. (*He is tired.*)
ona (f)	**jest**	*she is*	**Ona jest** ________. (*She is tired.*)
ono	**jest**	*it is*	**Ono jest** ________. (*It is tired.*)
pan (m) **pani** (f)	**jest**	*you (sir, madam) are*	**Pan jest** ________. (*You (sir) are tired.*) **Pani jest** ________. (*You (madam) are tired.*)

2 PLURAL

Polish		English	Example
my	**jesteśmy**	*we are*	**Jesteśmy zmęczeni/ zmęczone.** (*We are tired.*)
wy	**jesteście**	*you are*	**Jesteście zmęczeni/ zmęczone.** (*You are tired.*)
oni	**są**	*they are*	**Oni są zmęczeni.** (*They are tired.*)
one	**są**	*they are*	**One są zmęczone.** (*They are tired.*)
panowe	**są**	*gentlemen are*	**Panowie są zmęczeni.** (*You are tired, gentlemen.*)
panie	**są**	*ladies are*	**Panie są zmęczone.** (*You are tired, ladies.*)
państwo	**są**	*you (ladies and gentlemen) are*	**Państwo są zmęczeni.** (*You are tired, ladies and gentlemen*).

Listen and understand

01.06 **Listen to these words again and repeat. Then read the words out loud in Polish and English.**

problem (*problem*)
kot (*cat*)
lampa (*lamp*)
katedra (*cathedral*)
okno (*window*)
radio (*radio*)
telefon (*phone*)
komputer (*computer*)
mama (*mum*)
tata (*dad*)
brat (*brother*)
numer (*number*)
dokument (*document*)
mapa (*map*)
plan (*plan*)
dom (*house*)
bilet (*ticket*)

Go further

PROFESSIONS, NATIONALITIES AND CONDITIONS

01.07 **1 Listen and repeat the expressions.**

Nationalities		Professions		Conditions	
(m) Anglik **(f) Angielka**	*English*	**(m) lekarz** **(f) lekarka**	*doctor*	**(m) zmęczony** **(f) zmęczona**	*tired*
(m) Szkot **(f) Szkotka**	*Scottish*	**(m) aktor** **(f) aktorka**	*actor*	**(m) głodny** **(f) głodna**	*hungry*
(m) Walijczyk **(f) Walijka**	*Welsh*	**(m) student** **(f) studentka**	*student*	**(m) zajęty** **(f) zajęta**	*busy*
(m) Irlandczyk **(f) Irlandka**	*Irish*	**(m) artysta** **(f) artystka**	*artist*	**(m) pracowity** **(f) pracowita**	*hardworking*
(m) Polak **(f) Polka**	*Polish*	**(m) dziennikarz** **(f) dziennikarka**	*journalist*	**(m) dobry** **(f) dobra**	*good*
(m) Kanadyjczyk **(f) Kanadyjka**	*Canadian*	**(m) menadżer** **(f) menadżerka**	*manager*	**(m) szczęśliwy** **(f) szczęśliwa**	*happy*
(m) Argentyńczyk **(f) Argentynka**	*Argentinian*	**(m) programista** **(f) programistka**	*programmer*	**(m) smutny** **(f) smutna**	*sad*
(m) Niemiec **(f) Niemka**	*German*	**(m) nauczyciel** **(f) nauczycielka**	*teacher*	**(m) mądry** **(f) mądra**	*clever*

2 Add the narodowość (*nationality*) and zawód (*profession*) in Polish for these people:

Example: Ewa – Polish, doctor – *Polka/lekarka*

a Adam – English, student __________
b Josh – Canadian, artist __________
c Ingrid – Argentinian, journalist __________

Test yourself

1 01.08 **Say the sentences in Polish. Listen to the recording to check your answers and practice pronunciation.**

a Good morning/afternoon.
b Pleased to meet you.
c I'm Maria Grajewska.
d Please come in.
e Please sit down.
f Are you tired, sir?

2 **Choose the correct form to complete the sentences.**

a Maria is Polish. Is she (**Polską/Polką/Polak**)?
b Maria invites Andrew to come in. Does she say (**Proszę wejść/ Proszę wyjść/Proszę usiąść**)?

3 **Convert the sentences into negative ones.**

a Jestem głodny. ________
b On jest zmęczony. ________

4 01.09 **Respond in Polish to the questions and statements. Listen to the prompts in English.**

	Questions/Statements	Your response
a	**Dzień dobry, jestem Ewa Borowska.**	*Pleased to meet you.*
b	**Proszę usiąść.**	*Thank you.*
c	**Czy jest pan zmęczony?**	*Yes, a bit.*
d	**Czym się pan zajmuje?**	*I'm retired.*

SELF CHECK

	I CAN...
○	... introduce myself.
○	... state my nationality and profession.
○	... greet somebody in Polish.
○	... address somebody politely.
○	... say I'm hungry and tired.

2

In this unit you will learn how to:

» introduce others.
» talk about family.
» ask and answer questions about personal details.
» describe people and animals.

To jest mój pies, Azor

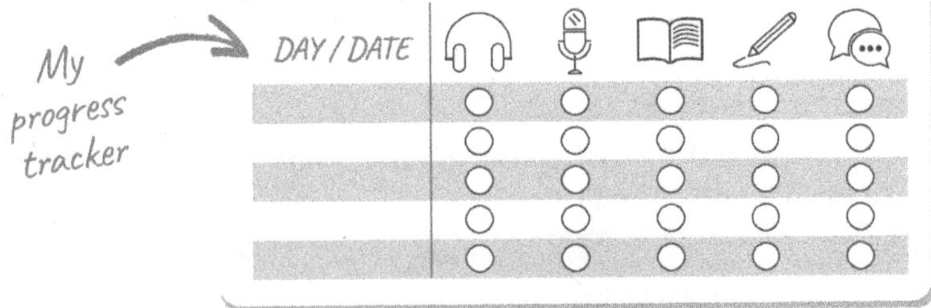

Pets in Poland

The Polish word for *pet* is **zwierzę domowe** (literally *domestic animal*), but many people use the more affectionate term **zwierzak domowy** or just **zwierzak** when talking about pets.

In residential areas in Poland, you may see notices on gates saying:

UWAGA! (*ATTENTION*) **ZŁY PIES!**

These inform visitors that a dog is present on the premises.

Under Communism, many people lived in small flats on large housing estates, so **małe zwierzęta** (*small animals*) such as a **kot** (*cat*), **chomik** (*hamster*), or **ryby** (*fish*) in **akwarium** (*aquarium*) were, and still are, popular. Others live in larger houses with gardens and can have larger pets, such as big dogs. The **owczarek niemiecki** (*German Shepherd*) is popular, and a well known Polish breed is **owczarek podhalański.**

Can you figure out what zły pies means? Which word literally means *sheepdog* – either of Germany or Podhale (an area in southern Poland)?

Vocabulary builder

02.01 **Listen as you look at the words and phrases and complete the English translations. Then listen again and try to imitate the speakers.**

DESCRIBING ANIMALS

to jest	________
pies	________
dobry	________
zły	________

NEW EXPRESSIONS

to jest (być)	*this is, it's (to be)*
mój	*my (used with masc. nouns)*
moja	*my (fem.)*
pies	*dog*
zły	*bad, angry, malicious (here: aggressive)*
dobry	*good*
nie	*no*
rodzina	*family*
żona	*wife*
dziadek	*grandfather*
wysoka (wysoki)	*tall*
córka	*daughter*
studentką (studentka)	*female student*
studiuje (studiować)	*s/he studies*
medycynę (medycyna)	*medicine*
Kto to jest?	*Who is it?*
ojciec	*father*

Match the English to the Polish.

zły studiuje dobry medycynę rodzina

- **a** doctor
- **b** not good
- **c** mother
- **d** a way to learn
- **e** not bad

Conversations

02.02 *Andrew and Maria are talking about Andrew's family. Suddenly Andrew hears a noise. He turns round and sees a dog coming into the living room. Maria explains that it's her dog, Azor.*

1 Is Azor an aggressive dog?

Maria	To jest mój pies, Azor.
Andrew	Czy to jest zły pies?
Maria	Nie! Azor to jest bardzo dobry pies.

02.03 *Andrew and Maria resume their conversation.*

2 Who are Molly and Thomas?

Andrew	To jest moja rodzina. Moja żona, Jenny.
Maria	Jest bardzo ładna.
Andrew	A to jest moja córka, Molly. Jest studentką.
Maria	Co studiuje?
Andrew	Medycynę.
Maria	A kto to jest?
Andrew	To jest mój ojciec, Thomas.

3 Now read the conversations and answer the questions.

- **a** How does Maria introduce Azor?
- **b** How would you ask a dog owner if their dog is aggressive?
- **c** What does Molly study?
- **d** What is Andrew's father's name?
- **e** What does **Kto to jest** mean?

4 Are these sentences correct? Answer Yes or No.

- **a** To jest moja córka Molly.
- **b** Jestem Andrew.
- **c** Maria jestem emerytką.
- **d** Jenny jesteś ładna.

Language discovery

Find the words in the conversations to complete the sentences.

- **a** Jenny to moja ________.
- **b** Molly nie jest ________. Ona jest studentką.
- **c** ________ to jest? To jest mój ojciec.

1 YOU KNOW WHO I'M TALKING ABOUT

Because Polish verbs have a unique ending for each person, **jestem** for *I*, **jesteś** for *you*, **jest** for *s/he, it* and so on, it's not necessary to use a personal pronoun (e.g., *I, you, he, she*, etc.) to know who you're talking about. That's why we can say about Andrew: **Jest głodny** (*He's hungry*). We don't have to use **on** (*he*), as **jest** is an **on/ona/ono** (*s/he/it*) form and the masculine form of the adjective **głodny** (*hungry*) clearly indicates a male.

2 THIS IS

When you use the Polish word **to**, corresponding to English *this, that* or *it* with **jest** (or other forms of **być**) and a noun, the noun stays in the basic form (traditionally called the nominative). For example, **To jest detektyw** (*This is a detective*).

In fact, it's not unusual for **jest** to be left out, leaving just **to** and a nominative as in **To angielski detektyw** (*This (is) an English detective*).

Why then does a word like **detektyw** stay in its basic form in the sentence: **To jest detektyw** (*This is a detective*) and changes when you say **Andrew jest detektywem** (*Andrew is a detective*)? It happens because in these two sentences **detektyw** plays a different role. In the first sentence you simply 'point and name' a noun. In the second sentence **detektyw** is used to complement (complete the meaning of) **być** (*to be*). In other words, in the first case **detektyw** complements **to** and if you omit **jest** you will still understand the meaning of the sentence. In the second case **detektyw** complements **jest** and the sentence is not complete if one of them is omitted. Traditionally, the form (or case) of the noun which plays this role is called instrumental.

Practice

1 Who is speaking? Put M for a man, F for a woman.

a Jestem zmęczona.
b Jestem emerytem.
c Jestem głodny.
d Jestem studentką.

2 Can jest be omitted? Put Yes or No.

a To jest Julia.
b On jest emerytem.
c Kasia jest studentką.
d Andrew to jest detektyw.

3 Replace the subject (name) with a pronoun (I, he, she, etc.) and insert the new sentence.

Example: Maria jest emerytką. *Ona jest emerytką.*

a Molly jest studentką.
b Andrew jest detektywem.
c Jenny i Molly są Angielkami. (English women)

4 Whose dog is it? Look at the possessive pronouns in the table.

Person (1st, 2nd, 3rd), Singular or Plural	Masculine	Feminine	Example sentence
ja	**mój**	**moja**	**mój pies/moja córka** *my dog/my daughter*
ty (familiar)	**twój**	**twoja**	**twój pies/twoja córka** *your dog/your daughter*
on, ona, **pan, pani** (polite for m/f)	**jego** **pana**	**jej** **pani**	**jego pies/jej córka*** *his dog/her daughter* **pana pies/pani córka**
my	**nasz**	**nasza**	**nasz pies/nasza córka** *our dog/our daughter*
wy (familiar)	**wasz**	**wasza**	**wasz pies/wasza córka** *your dog/your daughter*
oni, one **panowie** **panie** **państwo**	**ich** **panów** **państwa**	**ich** **pań**	**ich pies/ich córka** **panów pies/pań córka** **państwa pies/państwa córka** *their dog/their daughter* *your (gentlemen) dog/your (ladies) daughter* *your (ladies and gentlemen) dog/daughter*

* **Note:** In Polish, third person singular and plural is indeclinable, so you can say:

his dog – **jego pies**
his daughter – **jego córka**
their dog – **ich pies** (both masc. and fem.)

her dog – **jej pies**
her daughter – **jej córka**
their daughter – **ich córka**

Pronunciation

02.04 **Polish has nine vowels: a, ą, e, ę, i, o, ó, u, y.**

The more vowels in a word the easier it is to pronounce.

1 Listen and repeat:

- (**a**): **mapa** (*map*), **karta** (*menu*), **Ala** (female name), **lalka** (*doll*)
- (**e**): **Ewa** (*Eve*), **meta** (*finish*), **Europa** (*Europe*), **energia** (*energy*), **emerytka** (*retired female*)
- (**i**): **bigos** (*hunters' stew*), **Irena** (*female name*), **i** (*and*), **igła** (*needle*)
- (**o**): **pot** (*sweat*), **policja** (*police*), **pogotowie** (*emergency service*), **poczta** (*post office*), **lokal** (*premises*), **mleko** (*milk*), **woda** (*water*), **sok** (*juice*)
- (**ó** and **u**): **kubek** (*mug*), **ulica** (*street*), **ósemka** (8), **mucha** (*fly*)
- (**y**): **myć** (*to wash*), **być** (*to be*), **etykieta** (*etiquette*), **detektyw** (*detective*)
- (**ą** and **ę**): **się** (ś-e) (*oneself*), **będę** (bende) (*I will be*), **parę** (pa-re) (*a pair*), **kępę** (kempe) (*a clump*).

2 Read the words out loud with the English translations.

3 Now listen again and insert the correct words. Cover up the list in Exercise 1.

English	Polish
map	
sweat	
Europe	
emergency service	
menu	
post office	

4 Which Polish vowels did you pronounce in Exercise 3?

Conversation

02.05 *Andrew looks at the photographs on the wall. He asks Maria who the people in them are.*

1 Who is Jakub?

Andrew	Kto to jest?
Maria	To jest mój dziadek, Tomasz.
Andrew	A to?
Maria	To jest moja mama, Teresa.
Andrew	A to? Kto to jest?
Maria	To jest mój ojciec, Jakub.

2 Find the words in the conversation that mean:

a mum
b father
c grandfather

3 Now read the conversation and answer the questions.

a What is Maria's grandfather's name?
b How does Maria introduce her mum?
c How would you ask *who is this*?

4 What do you think? To introduce your wife you would say:

a To jest moja córka.
b To jest moja żona.
c To jest mój ojciec.

Practice

1 Find possessive phrases in the conversation and insert mój or moja as appropriate.

Example: *moja rodzina my family*

a ________ mama
b ________ córka
c ________ ojciec
d ________ dziadek
e ________ brat

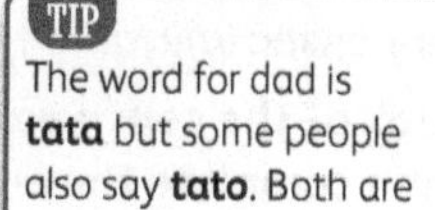
TIP
The word for dad is **tata** but some people also say **tato**. Both are masculine.

2 Match the pronouns on the left with nouns on the right.

a mój	pies
b moja	ojciec
c twój	mama
d twoja	córka

3 Translate these sentences into Polish.

a This is his dog.
b This is her daughter.
c This is your father.
d This is my brother.

4 Say the sentences in Exercise 3 in Polish.

5 Now introduce a friend's family in Polish. Use your best pronunciation.

Go further

MÓJ AND *MOJA*

In Polish, gender affects nouns and adjectives but also pronouns.

mój = masculine	**moja** = feminine	**moje** = neuter
mój ojciec (*my father*)	**moja rodzina** (*my family*)	**moje radio** (*my radio*)

Look at the conversations in this unit. Find other possessive phrases then complete the equations:

________ + ________ = a possessive phrase with a masculine noun

________ + ________ = a possessive phrase with a feminine noun

________ + ________ = a possesive phrase with neuter noun

COMPLETING THE MEANING OF ANDREW

Remember these sentences? **To jest detektyw./Andrew jest detektywem.**

In the second sentence, the noun **detektywem** is in the instrumental case. That is, it shows that it is the instrument by which the subject accomplishes something. Thus, the word **detektywem** completes the meaning of Andrew.

Look at the ways to form nouns in the instrumental case:

- Masculine nouns (ending in a consonant) add **-em** (or **-iem** if they end in **-g** or **-k**):

student	(*male student*)	**studentem**
Polak	(*Polish man*)	**Polakiem**

- Feminine (and some masculine exceptions) nouns ending in **-a** change to **-ą**:

studentka	(*female student*)	**studentką**
córka	(*daughter*)	**córką**

Neuter nouns lose their final **-o/-e** in favor of **-em** (or **-iem** after **-g** and **-k**):

piwo	(*beer*)	**piwem**
radio	(*radio*)	**radiem**

Mark the nouns that are in the instrumental case.

a radiem
b emerytka
c studentką
d Polakiem
e piwo

Test yourself

1 Say the sentences in Polish.

a This is my dog, Toffee.
b He's a very good dog.
c Is this your (**twoja**) family?
d Yes, it's my wife and daughter.
e She's very pretty.
f Molly's a student.
g She studies medicine.
h Who's this?
i This is my grandfather, Jakub.
j Is this your mum?
k What is it?
l This is my family.

2 Complete the sentences.

a Moja córka jest (medycyna/ładna/zły).
b To jest moja (córka/pies/emerytką).
c Ona studiuje (ojciec/mama/medycynę).
d Azor to bardzo dobry (uwaga/dziadek/pies).

3 How many family members can you introduce in Polish? Introduce them now.

4 02.06 **Respond in Polish to the questions and statements. Listen to the recording to check your answers and practice pronunciation.**

	Questions/Statements	Your response
a	**Kto to jest?**	*This is my father.*
b	**Co studiuje twoja córka?**	*She studies medicine.*
c	**To jest mój ojciec.**	*Pleased to meet you.*
d	**Czy to jest zły pies?**	*No, it's a good dog.*

SELF CHECK

	I CAN...
○	... introduce others.
○	... talk about family.
○	... ask and answer questions about personal details.
○	... describe people and animals.

3

In this unit you will learn how to:
- say you have or haven't got something.
- ask and answer questions about relationships.
- talk about things you have.
- talk about things you do.

Jestem szczęśliwy – mam czas i pieniądze

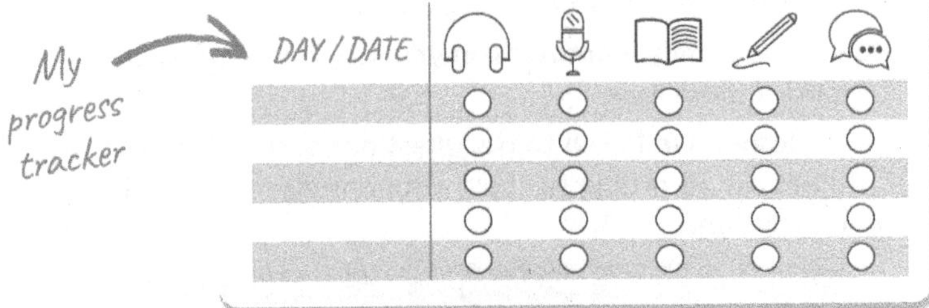

Family life in Poland

Family is important to Polish people. When you ask a Polish person **Czy masz rodzinę?** (*Have you got a family?*), they might refer to **dzieci** (*children*), **rodzice** (*parents*), **rodzeństwo** (*siblings*), **dziadkowie** (*grandparents*), and **kuzyni** (*cousins*), sometimes many times removed. It is not uncommon in Poland to meet families with a less traditional make-up, including blended families or families that have members from different cultures or different countries. Poland has been rather secular in recent decades but people still celebrate culturally Catholic holidays – **Boże Narodzenie** (*Christmas*), **Wielkanoc** (*Easter*) or **Wszystkich Świętych** (*All Saints' Day*).

Can you guess which group of relatives (rodzice, rodzeństwo or dziadkowie) dziadek belongs to?

Vocabulary builder

03.01 Listen as you look at the words and complete the English translations. Then listen again and try to imitate the speakers.

BORROWED WORDS

fotografie (fotografia) __________
kontakty (kontakt) __________
adresu (adres) __________
architektem (architekt) __________

Like English, Polish has many words borrowed from other languages such as Greek, Latin and French.

NEW EXPRESSIONS

ma (mieć)	*(s/he/it) has*
w (+ locative)	*(located) in*
chyba	*I think, I suppose*
jaki	*what (sort of)*
ani ... ani ...	*neither ... nor ...*
nazwiska (nazwisko)	*surname*
To żaden problem.	*It's no problem at all.*
archiwum (neuter)	*archive(s)*
czas na + acc.	*time for*
herbatę (herbata)	*tea*
dużo	*a lot (of)*
rodzinne (rodzinny)	*family (adj.)*
męża (mąż)	*husband*
syna (syn)	*son*
dobrą pracę (dobra, praca)	*a good job*
pieniądze (plural)	*money*
dzieci (dziecko)	*children*
imię	*first name*
na emeryturze (na, emerytura)	*retired*
rozwiedzeni	*divorced (plural)*
rozwiedziona (f)/rozwiedziony (m)	*divorced (singular)*
przyrodnia siostra	*step-sister*
przyrodni brat	*step-brother*
partner (m)/partnerka (f)	*partner*

The Polish words for 'step-mum' (**macocha**) and 'step-dad' (**ojczym**) are outdated and have rather negative connotations. Unfortunately, there is no modern equivalent. Most people simply avoid those words and refer to their step-parents in different ways depending on their individual relationship/ situation.

Find the new expression that means:

a location; as in **in Polsce** (*in Poland*)
b first name
c last name

Conversation

03.02 *Maria needs to get together more information about Andrew's family. Andrew hasn't had much luck looking for his Polish family online. Maria asks if he's got time to stay a bit longer.*

1 What are two things Andrew hasn't got?

Maria	Czy ma pan rodzinę w Polsce?
Andrew	Chyba tak, ale mam problem.
Maria	Jaki problem?
Andrew	Nie mam ani nazwiska, ani adresu.
Maria	To żaden problem. Mam kontakty w Archiwum.
	Czy ma pan jeszcze czas na herbatę?
Andrew	Tak, mam dużo czasu.
Maria	Czy ma pan jakieś rodzinne dokumenty?
Andrew	Tak, mam. Proszę, to są dokumenty i fotografie.
Maria	Dziękuję.

2 Read the conversation and answer the questions.

- **a** Has Andrew got time for tea?
- **b** Has Andrew got any family documents with him?
- **c** How would you say 'I have contacts at the archive (office)'?
- **d** What does **To żaden problem** mean?

3 The lion is NOT saying To żaden problem! Can you guess what he is saying?

Language discovery

Complete the sentences with mam or ma.

a Robert ________ rodzinę.
b Ja ________ czas.
c Czy ________ pan adres?
d Ona ________ córkę.

1 IT'S NOT A PROBLEM

Żaden means *no, not a single, not any, none at all* and is frequently used in colloquial Polish. Look at these phrases using **żaden**.

za <u>żadne</u> pieniądze/skarby	*no way* *not for all the tea in China* *(literally: for no money/treasures)*
Jan nie ma <u>żadnych</u> przyjaciół.	*John has no friends at all.*
pod <u>żadnym</u> pozorem	*under no circumstances* *(literally: under no appearance)*

2 MORE ABOUT INTRODUCTIONS: *MY HUSBAND'S NAME IS PETER*

Maria says, **Mój mąż ma na imię Piotr.** This is the second way to introduce yourself or someone else when using just the first name. Look at these examples.

I	**Mam na imię James.**	*My (first) name's James.*
you	**Jak masz na imię?**	*What's your first name?*
he	**Ma na imię Kacper.**	*His name's Kacper.*
she	**Ma na imię Oksana.**	*Her name's Oksana.*
you (polite)	**Pan ma na imię Igor? Pani ma na imię Anna?**	*Is your first name Igor? Is your first name Anna?*

3 MIEĆ

In Polish **mieć** is used to express possession:

Mam czas. *I have time.*

Mam samochód. *I have a car.*

It is also used to state age and say what you fancy:

Mam dwadzieścia lat. *I am twenty (years old).*

Lena ma ochotę na spacer. *Lena fancies a walk.*

4 THE HAVES AND THE HAVE NOTS

03.03 **The verb mieć *to have* looks like this in the present tense:**

Person (1st, 2nd, 3rd...), Singular or Plural	Polish	English	Example sentence
ja	**mam**	*I have*	**Mam rodzinę.** *I have a family.*
ty (familiar)	**masz**	*you have*	**Masz rodzinę.** *You have a family.*
on, ona, ono **pan, pani** (polite for m/f)	**ma**	*he/she/it has* *you have*	**On ma rodzinę.** *He has a family.*
my	**mamy**	*we have*	**Mamy rodzinę.** *We have a family.*
wy (familiar)	**macie**	*you have*	**Macie rodzinę.** *You have a family.*
oni, one **panowie** **panie** **państwo**	**mają**	*they have* *gentlemen have* *ladies have* *ladies and gentlemen have*	**Oni mają rodzinę.** *They have a family.*

Choose the correct form to complete the sentences.

a Tatiana (masz/ma/mam) syna.

b Czy (masz/ma/mam) dobrą pracę?

c Tak, (masz/ma/mam).

d Czy (masz/ma/mam) pani ochotę na herbatę?

e Ile on (masz/ma/mam) lat?

Pronunciation

CONSONANTS: SOFT AND HARD

Polish consonants: b, c, ć, d, f, g, h, j, k, l, ł, m, n, ń, p, r, s, ś, t, w, z, ź, ż

03.04 Consonants in Polish are complex but here are the basics. Consonants can be divided into two groups: soft and hard.

1 Listen and repeat.

SOFT CONSONANTS: ć, ń, ś, ź

Generally, a soft consonant has an accent above the letter.

ćma (*moth*)
koń (*horse*)
środek (*middle/centre*)
źródło (*spring/source*)

HARD CONSONANTS: **b, c, d, f, g, h, k, l, m, n, p, r, s, t, z, ż**

Hard consonants are not so hard when a vowel **-i-** gets involved. But that's another story, which will be told in Unit 4.

dobry (*good*)
pani (*lady*)
pan (*gentleman*)
bardzo (*very*)
fotografia (*photograph*)
żaden (*no, none*)
kontakty (*contacts*)
problem (*problem*)
archiwum (*archive*)
kto (*who*)
to (*this, it*)
medycyna (*medicine*)
studentka (f. *student*)
proszę (*please*)
wejść (*come in*)
trochę (*a bit*)
zmęczony (*tired*)
głodny (*hungry*)
klasa (*class/classroom*)
gazeta (*newspaper*)
dokument (*document*)
kawa (*coffee*)
córka (*daughter*)
żona (*wife*)
mama (*mum*)
brat (*brother*)
herbata (*tea*)

2 Read the words in Exercise 1 out loud with the English translations.

Conversation

03.05 *While Maria is looking through Andrew's documents, he asks her about her family.*

1 What is Maria's son's job?

Andrew	Czy pani ma rodzinę?
Maria	Tak, mam, męża i syna. To jest mój syn. Jest architektem. Ma dobrą pracę i pieniądze, ale nie ma dzieci.
Andrew	A pani mąż?
Maria	Mój mąż ma na imię Piotr. Też jest na emeryturze.

2 Read the conversation and answer the questions.

a Which members of her family does Maria talk about?

b What has Maria's son got?

c What hasn't he got?

d What is Maria's husband's name?

e What does he do for a living?

3 Read the conversation again and say it out loud.

4 Listen to the conversation again and fill in the blanks. Don't be discouraged if you need to listen a few times.

Czy ma pani ________ ?

Tak, ________ męża i ________ .

To jest mój ________ .

Ma dobrą ________ i pieniądze, ________ nie ma ________ .

Practice

1 Find the words in the conversation to complete the sentences. Use an appropriate form.

a Jestem ________ (*architect*).
b Mam ________ (*money*).
c Andrew nie ma ________ (*time*).
d Jakub ma ________ (*good job*).
e I have ________ (*husband and son*).

2 What's wrong? Find the errors then replace with the correct word(s).

a Mam dokumentu.
b Maria ma rodziny.
c Nie mam czas.
d Mam ochoty na herbatę.
e Ile mam pani lat?

3 Choose the correct form of the word to complete the sentences.

a Maria ma w Polsce (rodzina/rodzinę).
b Pan nie ma w Polsce (rodzina/rodziny).
c (Jaki/Jaka/Jakie) problem?
d (Jaki/Jaka/Jakie) fotografia?

Go further

MORE ABOUT HAVING: THE VERB *MIEĆ*

In Polish, you can't just have, you have to have 'something'. Look at the affirmative and negative forms. Notice that the direct object changes in negative form.

Affirmative	Negative
Mam dokument.	**Nie mam dokumentu.**
Andrew ma czas.	**Andrew nie ma czasu.**
Mam rodzinne fotografie.	**Nie mam rodzinnych fotografii.**

EXPRESSING POSSESSION, MEASURE AND SOURCE

Masculine nouns ending in a consonant typically add **-u** or **-a**.

czas/czasu **detektyw/detektywa** **kot/kota**

Feminine nouns typically change from **-a** to **-y**. Those which end **-ga** and **-ka** change to **-gi** and **-ki**.

żona (*wife*) **żonę** **żony**

Neuter nouns look much like masculine nouns, ending in **-a** instead of the **-o** or **-e**.

dziecko (*child*) **dziecko** **dziecka**

TIP

Imagine the verb **mieć** (*to have*) as a traveler who cannot travel alone – who must have a happy, positive companion or a grumpy, negative one.

1 Insert the words in Polish in an appropriate form.

Basic form	Affirmative	Negative
dokument	(a)	(b)
(c)	**dziecko**	(d)
(e)	(f)	**czasu**
pies	**psa**	(g)
(h)	**fotografię**	(i)

2 What do you think? Mark the correct sentence(s).

a Maria ma czasu.
b Mam żony.
c Nie mam dokumentu.

Test yourself

1 Say the sentences in Polish.

- **a** I've got family in Poland.
- **b** I've got a problem.
- **c** I fancy some tea.
- **d** Have you got any contacts at the archives?
- **e** I haven't got time.
- **f** I've plenty of time.
- **g** My daughter has a good job.
- **h** I have a dog, Rex.
- **i** I'm twenty years old.

2 03.06 **Respond in Polish to the questions and statements. Listen to the recording to check your answers and practice pronunciation.**

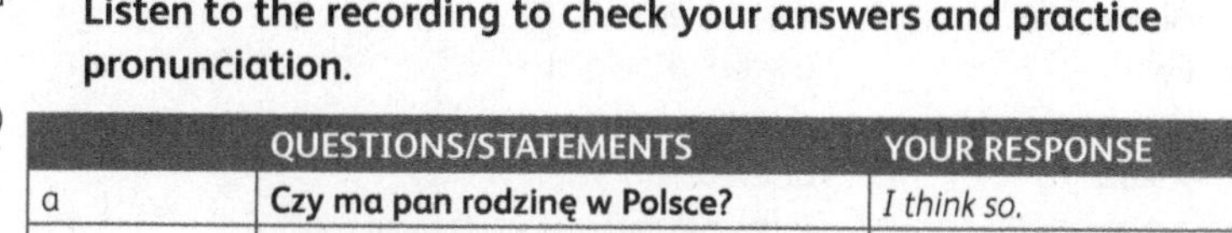

	QUESTIONS/STATEMENTS	YOUR RESPONSE
a	**Czy ma pan rodzinę w Polsce?**	*I think so.*
b	**Mam problem.**	*What sort of problem?*
c	**Czy ma pani czas na herbatę?**	*Yes, I've got lots of time.*
d	**Czy ma pan ochotę na herbatę?**	*Yes I have.*

3 Turn the sentences into negative ones. Use the correct grammar.

- **a** Mam czas.
- **b** Mój syn jest architektem.
- **c** Mają psa.
- **d** To jest mój ojciec.

4 Read the answers. What are the questions?

Example: (A) Tak, mam czas na herbatę. (Q) *Czy masz/ma pan/pani czas na herbatę?*

- **a** (A) Jestem emerytką. (Q) ________
- **b** (A) To jest mój ojciec. (Q) ________
- **c** (A) Tak, mam dokumenty. (Q) ________
- **d** (A) Nie, Azor to dobry pies. (Q) ________

SELF CHECK

I CAN...
... say I have or haven't got something.
... ask and answer questions about relationships.
... talk about things I have.
... talk about things I do.

R1 Review 1

1 Choose the correct surname (masculine or feminine form) for each first name.

a Hanna	Kosiński/Kosińska
b Tomasz	Dąbrowski/Dąbrowska
c Aleksander	Kosiarski/Kosiarska
d Ewa	Kowalski/Kowalska
e Krzysztof	Jakubowski/Jakubowska
f Jakub	Paderewski/Paderewska
g Julia	Słomczyński/Słomczyńska
h Amelia	Jaworski/Jaworska

2 Translate the following into English.

a Jestem Kuba Kowalczyk.
b Bardzo mi miło.
c Nie jestem Polakiem. Jestem Anglikiem.
d Mam polskie korzenie.
e Andrzej jest emerytem.
f Maria jest Polką.
g Czym się pan zajmuje?

3 Who said it? Choose M for male or F for female.

a Jestem zmęczony.
b Jestem zmęczona.
c Jestem emerytem.
d Jestem emerytką.
e Jestem Walijczykiem.
f Jestem Irlandką.

4 Choose the correct words to complete each sentence.

a mój pies/moim psem	To jest ______ .
b mój kot/moim kotem	To jest ______ .
c moja rodzina/moją rodziną	To jest ______ .
d Jest/To jest	______ moja córka.
e medycyna/medycynę	Studiuje ______ .
f studentem/studentką	Julia jest ______ .
g To/Ten Ania	______ , moja siostra.
h wysoki/wysoka	Anastazja jest ______ .
i wysoka dziewczyna/ wysoką dziewczyną	Zosia jest ______ .

j	miły/miłym (*nice*)	Krzysztof jest ______ .
k	to/ten	Krzysztof ______ miły mężczyzna.

5 Choose the correct words to complete each sentence.

a	rodzina/rodzinę	Maria ma w Polsce ______ .
b	rodzina/rodziny	Pan nie ma w Polsce ______ ?
c	Jaki/Jaka/Jakie	______ to problem?
d	Jaki/Jaka/Jakie	______ kot?
e	Żaden/Żadna/Żadne	______ fotografia
f	jakieś/jakichś	Czy ma pan przy sobie (*with/on you*) ______ dokumenty?
g	dokument/dokumenty fotografia/fotografie	To są ______ i ______ .
h	na/w/do	Państwo są ______ emeryturze?
i	adres/adresu	Przepraszam, nie mam ______ .
j	adres/adresu	Proszę, to jest ______ .
k	na/w/do	Pani ma ______ imię Agnieszka?
l	emerytka/emerytką	Moja mama jest ______.
m	emerytka/emeryt	Mój ojciec to ______ .
n	samochód/samochodu	Nie mamy ______ .

6 Look at the advert on a students' notice board and answer the questions.

a What is Tomek advertising?

b What does Tomek study?

Ogłoszenie

Jestem Tomek. Jestem studentem medycyny.
Mam wolny pokój.
Proszę zadzwonić pod numer tel 689 415 237

7 Look at the word endings. Which are masculine, feminine or neuter?

a lampa (*lamp*)
b samochód (*car*)
c radio (*radio*)
d telefon (*phone*)
e herbata (*tea*)
f kobieta (*woman*)
g dziecko (*child*)
h dom (*house*)
i autobus (*bus*)
j tramwaj (*tram*)
k tulipan (*tulip*)
l mapa (*map*)
m piwo (*beer*)

In this unit you will learn how to:

» tell the time and handle numbers.
» describe your plans.
» describe what you must/have to do or don't have to do.
» agree to meet someone.

Muszę już iść

My progress tracker → DAY / DATE

About time in Poland

Czas to pieniądz might be a popular saying in Poland, but you may notice many people's attitude to punctuality. **Kwadrans akademicki** is a common allowance given to people who are late. Traditionally that's how long **studenci** (*students*) would wait for a **profesor** (*professor*) who was late for class at **szkoła** (*school*) or **uniwersytet** (*university*) before disappearing.

In towns and cities, **południe** (*midday*) is often announced by church bells ringing. If you are in Kraków city center, you can hear a **hejnał** (*a bugle call*), played by a trumpeter every hour from the top of the tower of St Mary's Church in the main square. The 24-hour **zegar** (*clock*) is commonly used, for example in train announcements or when making appointments, but using the 12-hour clock also works. Many employees in companies based in Poland enjoy **elastyczny czas pracy** (*flexible working hours*). People often also work **zdalnie** (*remotely*) either part-time or full-time.

Can you guess the English equivalent of Czas to pieniądz? How many minutes does kwadrans akademicki last?

Vocabulary builder

04.01 **Listen as you look at the words and phrases and complete the missing words. Then listen again and try to imitate the speakers.**

TIME AND NECESSITY

koniecznie	_________, *absolutely (must)*
Muszę już iść.	*I _________ go.*
musi pan	*you _________ (polite to a man)*
_________	*then, next, afterwards*
wrócić _________ (wracać, wrócić)	*come/go back to*
_________ (załatwiać, załatwić)	*deal with, do, settle*

NEW EXPRESSIONS

spotkać znowu	*meet again*
przepraszam	*I apologize*
która	*which (who)*
dlaczego	*why*
kilka	*a few, several*
spraw (sprawa)	*thing, matter, problem*
wymienić (wymieniać > wymienić)	*change, exchange*
pieniądze (plural)	*money*
karta (płatnicza)	*(bank) card*
zadzwonić (dzwonić > zadzwonić)	*ring, phone to*
domu (dom)	*home, house*
hotelu (hotel)	*hotel*
rozpakować się (rozpakowywać się > rozpakować się)	*get unpacked*
zwiedzić (zwiedzać > zwiedzić)	*visit, go sightseeing in*
spotkać się (spotykać się > spotkać się)	*meet, get together*
znowu	*again*
bardzo chętnie	*would love to*

Did you notice? Which expressions could be on a list of things to do?

- **a** zwiedzić
- **b** bardzo chętnie
- **c** rozpakować się
- **d** dlaczego

Conversation

04.02 *Andrew looks at his watch. He realizes the battery is dead and that he has spent a few hours with Maria. He has to go now.*

1 What time do you think it is?

Andrew	Przepraszam, która godzina?
Maria	Czwarta.
Andrew	Niestety, muszę już iść.
Maria	Ojej, szkoda. Dlaczego musi pan iść?
Andrew	Muszę załatwić kilka spraw. Muszę wrócić do hotelu i rozpakować się. Potem muszę wymienić pieniądze i zadzwonić do domu.
Maria	Musi pan też zwiedzić Kraków.
Andrew	O tak, koniecznie.
Maria	Musimy spotkać się znowu.
Andrew	Tak. Bardzo chętnie.

2 Read the conversation and answer the questions.

- **a** Why does Andrew have to go?
- **b** Is Maria disappointed?
- **c** What does Maria suggest Andrew must do?
- **d** What does Andrew say to agree with her?
- **e** How do you say 'I'd love to' in Polish?
- **f** What does **niestety** mean?

3 Match the Polish and English.

a czwarta	**1** (I) have to
b pieniądze	**2** exchange
c wymienić	**3** 4:00
d muszę	**4** money
e musi pan	**5** (you) must

4 Listen to the conversation and speak along.

5 Listen to the conversation again and practice your pronunciation.

Language discovery

What do you say? If the sentences below are the answers, what are the questions?

a ________? Czwarta.
b ________? Muszę załatwić kilka spraw.
c ________? Tak, muszę zobaczyć Kraków.

1 TELLING THE TIME

To say what the time is, Polish speakers use *the ...th hour*:

English	Polish
first hour (1:00)	**pierwsza**
second hour (2:00)	**druga**
third hour (3:00)	**trzecia**
fourth hour (4:00)	**czwarta**
fifth hour (5:00)	**piąta**
sixth hour (6:00)	**szósta**
seventh hour (7:00)	**siódma**
eighth hour (8:00)	**ósma**
ninth hour (9:00)	**dziewiąta**
tenth hour (10:00)	**dziesiąta**
eleventh hour (11:00)	**jedenasta**
twelfth hour (12:00)	**dwunasta**

To say *It's one o'clock*, you can just say **pierwsza** or any of these forms:

Godzina pierwsza. **Jest godzina pierwsza.** **Jest pierwsza.**

2 THE VERB *MUSIEĆ*

English uses *must* and *have to*, but Polish only has the verb **musieć**. The good news is that verbs following **musieć** are always in the infinitive. The infinitive corresponds to the basic form of a verb that follows *to* in English. Indeed a lot of people like to include the *to*: *She likes to swim. To be or not to be?*

Study the table. This is how **musieć** is used in all persons:

Person (1st, 2nd, 3rd...), Singular or Plural	Polish	English	Example sentence
ja	**muszę**	*I must*	**Muszę zobaczyć Kraków.** *I must see Kraków.*
ty (familiar)	**musisz**	*you must*	**Musisz zobaczyć Kraków.** *You must see Kraków.*
on, ona, ono **pan, pani** (polite for m/f)	**musi**	*he/she/it must* *you must*	**On musi zobaczyć Kraków.** *He must see Kraków.*
my	**musimy**	*we must*	**Musimy zobaczyć Kraków.** *We must see Kraków.*
wy (familiar)	**musicie**	*you must*	**Musicie zobaczyć Kraków.** *You must see Kraków.*
oni, one **panowie** **panie** **państwo**	**muszą**	*they must* *gentlemen must* *ladies must* *ladies and gentlemen must*	**Oni muszą zobaczyć Kraków.** *They must see Kraków.*

3 *MUSTN'T* AND *DON'T HAVE TO*

In Polish **nie musisz** means you *don't have to*, meaning you are not obligated to.

Nie musisz jechać do Krakowa. *You don't have to go to Kraków.*

Nie muszę, ale chcę. *I don't have to, but I want to.*

Practice

1 Choose the correct word to complete the sentences.

a Dlaczego (musi/musicie) pani iść?

b Oni (muszę/muszą) już jechać (*go by car*).

c (Ty) nie (musisz/muszą) się od razu (*immediately*) rozpakować.

d A my (muszę/musimy) koniecznie zadzwonić do domu.

2 Translate the time into Polish: 1:00, 5:00, 6:00, 11:00

Pronunciation

THE DOUBLE LIFE OF *I*

04.03 **How to turn hard consonants into soft ones**

There is more to the vowel **i** than meets the eye. For example, the nouns **pani**, **archiwum** and **fotografia** all have a hard consonant (**n** in **pani**, **h** in **archiwum** and (second) **f** in **fotografia**), which is followed by **i**. This particular combination means that a hard consonant is no longer hard; it becomes soft just like the consonants with an accent.

If any of the soft consonants are followed by a vowel then an accent is replaced by **i**. However, the pronunciation stays the same.

1 Listen to the words and repeat.

ciało (*body*)
niebo (*sky*)
cierpieć (*to suffer*)
ziarno (*grain*)
widzieć (*to see*)
miska (*bowl*)
dni (*days*)
biały (*white*)
dzień (*day*)
dziki (*wild*)
sień (*hallway*)
łokieć (*elbow*)
cień (*shadow*)
pisklę (*chick*)
list (*letter*)
wiotki (*limp*)

2 Listen again and say these words in Polish. Cover up the list in Exercise 1.

a sky
b day
c elbow
d letter
e body
f white

3 Did you notice? Which consonants does *i* follow in the Polish words in Exercise 2?

Listen and understand

TELLING THE TIME

04.04 Listen and repeat.

1 Say it the long way.

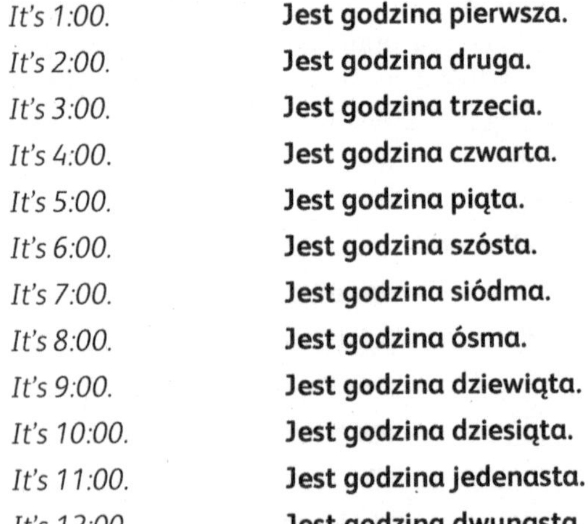

It's 1:00.	**Jest godzina pierwsza.**
It's 2:00.	**Jest godzina druga.**
It's 3:00.	**Jest godzina trzecia.**
It's 4:00.	**Jest godzina czwarta.**
It's 5:00.	**Jest godzina piąta.**
It's 6:00.	**Jest godzina szósta.**
It's 7:00.	**Jest godzina siódma.**
It's 8:00.	**Jest godzina ósma.**
It's 9:00.	**Jest godzina dziewiąta.**
It's 10:00.	**Jest godzina dziesiąta.**
It's 11:00.	**Jest godzina jedenasta.**
It's 12:00.	**Jest godzina dwunasta.**

2 Do you remember? Say it the short way.

a It's 3:00.
b It's 9:00.
c It's 2:00.

3 Translate the time into Polish.

a
Ines Excuse me. What's the time?
Dawid It's 7 p.m.

b
Vadim Excuse me. What's the time?
Natalia It's 4 p.m.

c
Jingyi Excuse me. What's the time?
Staś It's 10 p.m.

AT WHAT TIME

You have been learning how to tell the time. Time to move on to tell at what time something happens.

1 Look at the examples below then complete the remaining forms.

Która godzina?	What's the time?	**O której godzinie?**	At what time?
1:00	**pierwsza**	**O pierwszej.**	At 1:00.
2:00	**druga**	**O drugiej.**	At 2:00.
3:00	**trzecia**	**O trzeciej.**	At 3:00.
4:00	**czwarta**	**O** ________ .	
5:00	**piąta**	**O** ________ .	
6:00	**szósta**	**O** ________ .	
7:00	**siódma**	**O** ________ .	
8:00	**ósma**	**O** ________ .	
9:00	**dziewiąta**	**O** ________ .	
10:00	**dziesiąta**	**O** ________ .	
11:00	**jedenasta**	**O** ________ .	
12:00	**dwunasta**	**O** ________ .	

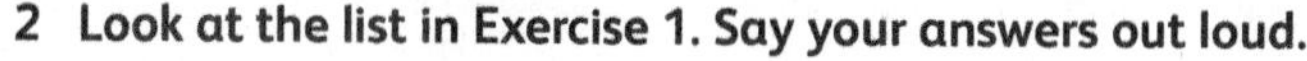

2 Look at the list in Exercise 1. Say your answers out loud.

3 Say your answers again. Pronounce the words carefully.

4 Answer the questions in Polish.

a When are we going? Say 'at 12:00'.

b When do we meet? Say 'at 6:00'.

c When is he speaking? Say 'at 7:00'.

Go further

REFLEXIVE ACTIONS

Polish shows actions we perform on ourselves or to each other by using reflexive verbs. It's easy to recognize a reflexive verb by **się**.

The word **się** is used for *myself, yourself, himself, herself, itself, ourselves, yourself* and *themselves*:

Spotykam się z bratem.	*I meet my brother.*
Spotykasz się z bratem.	*You meet your brother.*
Spotykają się z bratem.	*They meet their brother.*
Myję się.	*I'm washing (myself).*
Golę się.	*I'm shaving (myself).*
pakować się	*to pack (your things or your bags, not yourself)*
rozpakować się	*to unpack (your things or your bags, not yourself)*

Się is used with the **pan/pani**-words in polite address:

Jak często pan(i) się spotyka z bratem?	*How often do you meet your brother?*

It's worth remembering that not all Polish reflexive verbs have counterparts in English.

THE WORD SIĘ

The word **się** can go after, before, or separate from the verb it refers to. The change of order is dictated by the rhythm of the sentence, and it does not alter the meaning.

Musimy spotkać się znowu = Musimy się spotkać znowu. = Musimy się znowu spotkać.

1 **Reorder the sentence according to the model above.**
   - **a** Muszę się rozpakować w hotelu.
   - **b** On musi golić się codziennie. (*every day*)
   - **c** Ona musi się myć rano. (*in the morning*)

2 **Put the words in any correct order.**
   - **a** się/muszę/rozpakować
   - **b** muszą/Maria/ Kraków/i/Andrew/zwiedzić
   - **c** godzina/przepraszam/która

Test yourself

1 Say the sentences in Polish.

a I've got to go.
b Why do you have to go?
c She has to return to her (**jej**) hotel.
d I've got to phone home.
e You must see London (**Londyn**).
f We have to meet again.
g I'd love to.
h Oh yes, absolutely.

2 04.06 **Respond in Polish to the questions and statements. Listen to the recording to check your answers and practice pronunciation.**

	QUESTIONS/STATEMENTS	YOUR RESPONSE
a	**Musimy spotkać się znowu.**	*I'd love to.*
b	**Musi pani zwiedzić Kraków.**	*Oh yes, absolutely.*
c	**Muszę już iść.**	*Pity.*
d	**Czy masz trochę czasu?**	*Yes, I have.*
e	**Poproszę nazwisko.**	________

3 Complete the sentences.

a O której godzinie się spotkamy? O (4:00) ________ .
b Andrew musi rozpakować ________ .
c Ewa musi wymienić ________ .
d Przepraszam, która ________ ?
e Tomek musi załatwić kilka ________ .

SELF CHECK

I CAN...

- ... tell the time and handle numbers.
- ... describe my plans.
- ... describe what I must/have to do.
- ... or don't have to do.
- ... agree to meet someone.

5

In this unit you will learn how to:

» ask how someone is.
» ask for help and information.
» say numbers 0–100.
» say you would or wouldn't like to do something.

Chciał(a)bym zamówić stolik

My progress tracker

DAY / DATE					
	○	○	○	○	○
	○	○	○	○	○
	○	○	○	○	○
	○	○	○	○	○
	○	○	○	○	○

Visiting Poland

Polish people have **duma** (*pride*) in their history, **piękny krajobraz** (*beautiful landscapes*) and **bogate dziedzictwo kulturowe** (*rich cultural heritage*). If you search online or visit **informacja turystyczna** you will find that Poland has 23 national parks, the last primeval forest in Europe in Białowieża, sand dunes, gold, salt and coal **kopalnie**, and is the birth place of Fryderyk Chopin and Maria Skłodowska-Curie. Destinations include: Kraków; the capital Warszawa; Gdańsk in the north with unique architecture, interesting history and coastal towns; and Zakopane in the south near the stunning **Tatry** (*Tatra*) mountains.

Poland's culture has been influenced by Ukraine and Jewish culture. Art enthusiasts will enjoy the many galleries, museums and music venues. For sports enthusiasts, there is also **jazda konna** (*horse riding*), **żeglarstwo** (*sailing*), **kolarstwo** (*cycling*), **chodzenie** (*walking*) and **zwiedzanie zabytków** (*sightseeing*).

Do these words sound familiar: informacja turystyczna and kopalnie? Can you guess what they mean?

Vocabulary builder

05.01 **Listen as you look at the words and complete the English translations. Then listen again and try to imitate the speakers.**

BORROWED WORDS

recepcja	________
restauracja	________
informacja	________
transformacja	________

NEW EXPRESSIONS

spotkanie	*meeting, get together*
nie ma za co	*you're welcome, not at all*
dziękuję za (dziękować > podziękować)	*thank you for*
znaleźć (znajdować > znaleźć)	*find*
do zobaczenia	*see you*
jutro	*tomorrow*
słucham (słuchać)	*Hello, I'm listening; can I help you?*
zamówić (zamawiać > zamówić)	*to order, to book*
stolik	*table in a restaurant, small table*
na którą godzinę (która godzina)	*For what time; when for?*
poproszę (prosić > poprosić)	*please (extra polite); can I have ... please*
do widzenia	*goodbye (till we see each other)*
pokój	*room*
mówi (mówić > powiedzieć)	*is speaking, speaks*
Co słychać?	*How are things? What's new?*
z + instrumental; z tobą (ty)	*with; with you*
potrzebuję pomocy (potrzebować pomoc)	*I need help.*
zasięgnąć informacji (zasięgać > zasięgnąć, informacje)	*get some information*
dobrze (dobry)	*OK, correctly, well, right*

Do you agree? Answer Yes or No.

a I'll ask **Co słychać?** to order a table in a restaurant.
b I'll say **nie ma za co** to let you know I can't meet tomorrow.
c **Poproszę** means *see you*.

Conversations

05.02 *Andrew is leaving Maria's apartment. Once again, he expresses his desire to track down his relatives.*

1 When are Andrew and Maria going to see each other again?

Andrew	Dziękuję za spotkanie.
Maria	Nie ma za co.
Andrew	Tak bardzo chciałbym znaleźć moją rodzinę.
Maria	Oczywiście, rozumiem. Do zobaczenia jutro.

05.03 *Andrew returns to his hotel. He has unpacked his things and he phones the reception desk.*

2 Why does Andrew call the receptionist?

Receptionist	Dzień dobry, recepcja. Słucham.
Andrew	Dzień dobry. Chciałbym zamówić stolik w restauracji.
Receptionist	Na którą godzinę?
Andrew	Na siódmą trzydzieści.
Receptionist	Poproszę nazwisko.
Andrew	Stewart.
Receptionist	Pan Andrew Stewart?
Andrew	Tak.
Receptionist	Pokój sto dwadzieścia pięć?
Andrew	Tak.
Receptionist	Proszę bardzo.
Andrew	Dziękuję bardzo. Do widzenia.

3 Read the conversations and answer the questions.

- **a** What does **nie ma za co** mean?
- **b** What does Maria say to confirm she understands?
- **c** What is Andrew room's number?
- **d** For what time would Andrew like to book a table?
- **e** What do you say when you answer the phone?
- **f** How would you greet a caller if you were a receptionist?
- **g** How would you ask *for what time* in Polish?

Language discovery

1 Look at the table.

	Która godzina? *What time?*	O której godzinie? *At what time?*	Na którą godzinę? *For what time?*
1:00	**pierwsza**	**o pierwszej**	**na pierwszą**
2:00	**druga**	**o drugiej**	**na drugą**
3:00	**trzecia**	**o trzeciej**	**na trzecią**
4:00	**czwarta**	**o czwartej**	**na czwartą**
5:00	**piąta**	**o piątej**	
6:00	**szósta**	**o szóstej**	
7:00	**siódma**	**o siódmej**	
8:00	**ósma**	**o ósmej**	
9:00	**dziewiąta**	**o dziewiątej**	
10:00	**dziesiąta**	**o dziesiątej**	
11:00	**jedenasta**	**o jedenastej**	
12:00	**dwunasta**	**o dwunastej**	

2 Did you notice the change in spelling in the word endings?

3 Try to figure out the remaining forms and complete the table.

1 *I WOULD LIKE* AND *I MUST/HAVE TO*

Chciał(a)bym (*I would like*) and **muszę** (*I must/have to*) behave grammatically in the same way when used with other verbs. The spelling/forms of their direct objects do not change.

You can substitute **chciał(a)bym** (*I would like*) and **muszę** (*I must/have to*) for all their uses in this and those in the previous unit:

Person: 1st person Singular (of would like – **chciałbym** (m.), **chciałabym** (f.))	Example sentence
I'd like + to go now.	**Chciał(a)bym + już iść.**
I have + to go now.	**Muszę + już iść.**
I'd like + to book a taxi.	**Chciał(a)bym + zamówić taksówkę.**
I have + to book a taxi.	**Muszę + zamówić taksówkę.**
I'd like + to exchange some money.	**Chciał(a)bym + wymienić pieniądze.**
I have + to exchange some money.	**Muszę + wymienić pieniądze.**
I'd like + to do some shopping.	**Chciał(a)bym + zrobić zakupy.**
I have + to do some shopping.	**Muszę + zrobić zakupy.**

Person (1st, 2nd, 3rd), Singular or Plural	Masculine	Feminine	Example sentence
ja	**chciałbym**	**chciałabym**	**Chciał(a)bym zamówić stolik.** *I'd like to book a table.*
ty (familiar)	**chciałbyś**	**chciałabyś**	**Chciał(a)byś zamówić stolik.** *You'd like to book a table.*
on, ona, pan, pani (polite for m/f)	**chciałby**	**chciałaby**	**On chciałby zamówić. stolik.** *He would like to book a table.*
my	**chcielibyśmy**	**chciałybyśmy**	**Chciałybyśmy zamówić stolik.** *We'd like to book a table.*
wy (familiar)	**chcielibyście**	**chciałybyście**	**Chcielibyście zamówić stolik.** *You'd like to book a table.*
oni, one panowie panie państwo	**chcieliby**	**chciałyby**	**Oni chcieliby zamówić stolik.** *They'd like to book a table.*

2 I WOULDN'T LIKE

On the other hand, **nie** used with verbs changes the case for the direct object noun and thus the spelling of the noun.

Subject	Verb	Direct object	Subject	Verb	Direct object
I	*would like to buy*	*a guide*	**(Ja)***	**chciał(a)bym kupić**	**przewodnik**
I	*wouldn't like to buy*	*a guide*	**(Ja)**	**nie chciał(a)bym kupić**	**przewodnika**

* When the subject is 'ja', it can usually be omitted, unless the speaker wants to emphasise specifically that it's them. (It's me who would like to buy it, not the other person.)

3 WHEN CASES COINCIDE

When two cases coincide in form, the change of the case may be hidden, and the spelling of the noun doesn't change.

Mam psa. (acc) — *I've got a dog.*

Nie mam psa. (gen) — *I haven't got a dog.*

Practice

1 Complete the sentences with time in the appropriate form.

- **a** Film zaczyna się (*starts*) o ________ (7:00).
- **b** Obiad jest o ________ (4:00).
- **c** Lekcja (*lesson*) zaczyna się o ________ (9:00).
- **d** Mecz zaczyna się o ________ (3:00).
- **e** Chciałbym zamówić taksówkę (*taxi*) na ________ (6:00).
- **f** Jestem umówiony (*got an appointment*) na ________ (1:00).
- **g** Jest godzina ________ (12:00).

2 Complete the sentences with a word from the box.

Kraków przewodnik informacji psa w Krakowie kot stolik informacja Wawelu Wawel

- **a** Chciałbym mieszkać ________.
- **b** Nie muszę zobaczyć ________.
- **c** Chciałabym zasięgnąć ________.
- **d** Chciałbym mieć ________.
- **e** Chciałbym zamówić ________.
- **f** Chciałabym kupić ________.

Listen and understand

1 05.04 **Listen to the conversation.**

Ewa	Słucham.
Maria	Cześć. Mówi Maria.
Ewa	Cześć. Co słychać?
Maria	Dziękuję, dobrze. Chciałabym spotkać się z tobą. Potrzebuję pomocy.
Ewa	Jakiej pomocy?
Maria	Chciałabym zasięgnąć informacji i znaleźć dokumenty.
Ewa	Dobrze.

2 What would Maria like to do? Listen again and mark the correct answer.

a find documents/find photographs

b meet Ewa/go home

3 Listen and complete Maria's missing words.

a Dziękuję, dobrze. Chciałabym spotkać ________ z tobą.

b ________ zasięgnąć ________ i znaleźć ________.

4 Match the verbs on the left with the nouns on the right as they appear in the conversation.

a potrzebuję	**1** informacji
b znaleźć	**2** z tobą
c zasięgnąć	**3** dokumenty
d spotkać się	**4** pomocy

CONSONANTS AND CONSONANTS

In Polish, some consonants form permanent partnerships with other consonants which together represent one sound: **ch**, **rz**, **sz**, **cz**, **dz**, **dż**, **dź**.

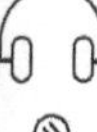

1 05.05 Listen and repeat.

chwila	*moment*
chętnie	*willingly*
trochę	*a bit*
chyba	*perhaps*
archiwum	*archive*
architekt	*architect*
chciałbym	*I'd like to*
rachunek	*check, bill*
kuchnia	*kitchen/cuisine*
schody	*stairs*
czas	*time*
deszcz	*rain*
dżokej	*jockey*
żona	*wife*
szkoła	*school*
szczur	*rat*
trzeba	*one needs to*
ryż	*rice*
kukurydza	*corn*
sadza	*soot*

2 Read the words out loud with the English translations.

3 Now listen again and give the Polish words. Cover up the list in Exercise 1.

a moment
b perhaps
c check
d willingly
e time
f school
g archive
h architect
i stairs
j kitchen
k rain
l rat

Go further

CARDINAL NUMBERS 0–1000

1 05.06 **Listen and repeat.**

0	**zero**	15	**piętnaście**
1	**jeden**	16	**szesnaście**
2	**dwa**	17	**siedemnaście**
3	**trzy**	18	**osiemnaście**
4	**cztery**	19	**dziewiętnaście**
5	**pięć**	20	**dwadzieścia**
6	**sześć**	30	**trzydzieści**
7	**siedem**	40	**czterdzieści**
8	**osiem**	50	**pięćdziesiąt**
9	**dziewięć**	60	**sześćdziesiąt**
10	**dziesięć**	70	**siedemdziesiąt**
11	**jedenaście**	80	**osiemdziesiąt**
12	**dwanaście**	90	**dziewięćdziesiąt**
13	**trzynaście**	100	**sto**
14	**czternaście**		

TIP

200	**dwieście**
300	**trzysta**
400	**czterysta**
500	**pięćset**
600	**sześćset**
700	**siedemset**
800	**osiemset**
900	**dziewięćset**
1000	**tysiąc**

Numbers in between 20 and 100 (and over 100) work in the same way as in English:

24	**dwadzieścia cztery**	78	**siedemdziesiąt osiem**
35	**trzydzieści pięć**	89	**osiemdziesiąt dziewięć**

Numbers used for telling the time are called ordinal numbers. Cardinal numbers answer the question: *how many?* (one, two, three, . . .) Ordinal numbers answer the question: *which one?* (first, second, third, etc.).

Polish speakers usually give out their mobile phone numbers as 3 groups of 3 digits each. Each group is read as a full number. For example: 602 is **sześćset dwa** (*six-hundred and two*), 854 is **osiemset pięćdziesiąt cztery** (*eight-hundred and fifty-four*).

2 Give the telephone numbers in words.

a 602 743 511

b 603 121 900

c 502 380 515

d 503 750 119

Test yourself

1 Say the sentences in Polish.

a Thank you for the meeting.
b I'd like to find my family.
c I'd like to book a table.
d Can I have your name, please?
e How are you?
f (For) what time?
g For seven thirty.
h I'd like to meet you.

2 Turn the sentences into negative ones.

a Chciałbym zamówić stolik.
b Chciałabym kupić przewodnik.
c Muszę zobaczyć Wawel.
d Mam konia.
e Chciałbym wymienić pieniądze.
f Muszę zrobić zakupy.
g Jestem głodny.

3 05.07 **Respond in Polish to the statements and questions. Listen to the audio to check your answers and practice pronunciation.**

	QUESTIONS/STATEMENTS	YOUR RESPONSE
a	**Potrzebuję pomocy.**	*What sort of help?*
b	**Chciałbym zamówić taksówkę.**	*Address, please.*
c	**Czy jest pan Amerykaninem?**	*No, I'm Scottish.*
d	**Chciałbym spotkać się z tobą.**	*At what time?*

SELF CHECK

	I CAN...
●	... say I would or wouldn't like to do something.
●	... ask how someone is.
●	... ask for help and information.
●	... say numbers 0–1000.

6

In this unit you will learn how to:

» ask for things politely.
» order food.
» ask for and pay the check.
» buy stamps and postcards.

Poproszę lody

My progress tracker

DAY / DATE					
	○	○	○	○	○
	○	○	○	○	○
	○	○	○	○	○
	○	○	○	○	○
	○	○	○	○	○

Foods and cuisine

Polish cuisine has been influenced by geography, climate, soil and history. The strong influence of German, Austrian, Hungarian, Jewish, French and Italian cuisine is one of the reasons why Polish cuisine is so varied. Bona Sforza, an Italian wife of King Zygmunt the Old, introduced **pomidory** (*tomatoes*). Henry de Valois – the first elected king of Poland – popularized French dishes. **Wołowina** (*beef*) was brought to Poland by Tartars who used to place raw meat under their saddle to tenderize it, giving us steak tartare.

Polish people like eating **zupy** (*soups*) such as **rosół** (*chicken stock soup*) and **barszcz** (*beetroot soup*). **Pierogi** (*the Polish relative of ravioli*) are also very popular.

The classic ingredient of Polish cuisine is **mięso**, usually **wieprzowina** (*pork*). Polish **szynka** (*ham*) is famous, and **kotlet schabowy** also known as **sznycel** (*schnitzel – breaded pork or veal chops*) are a main part of a traditional Sunday lunch. **Kuchnia wegetariańska** (*vegetarian cuisine*) and **kuchnia wegańska** (*vegan cuisine*) are also increasingly popular. The short-form **wege** can mean either, so it's worth checking before you order.

Can you name all types of mięso mentioned in the text?

Vocabulary builder

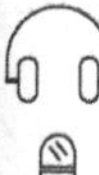

06.01 Listen as you look at the words and phrases and complete the English translations. Then listen again and try to imitate the speakers.

PAYING THE CHECK

Słucham państwa. ________?*
Poproszę rachunek. ________
Proszę bardzo. ________
Ile płacę? ________

*** literally:** *I'm listening to you, ladies and gentlemen*

NEW EXPRESSIONS

sernik	*cheesecake*	do + genitive	*to*
lody kawowe (lód, lody, kawowy)	*coffee ice cream*	do Wielkiej Brytanii (Wielka Brytania)	*for Great Britain*
a	*and (with a change of participant), and/but*	kelner(ka)	*server (m/f)*
		kobieta	*woman*
		sprzedawca	*(male) shop assistant*
		jestem wegetarianinem (wegetarianin)	*I'm vegetarian (m)*
zapłacić (płacić > zapłacić)	*pay*		
wykluczone (wykluczony)	*excluded, out of the question*	jestem wegetarianką (wegetarianka)	*I'm vegetarian (f)*
gościem (gość)	*guest*	jestem weganinem (weganin)	*I'm vegan (m)*
tę (ta)	*this*		
widokówka	*postcard*	jestem weganką (weganka)	*I'm vegan (f)*
znaczek	*stamp*		
zwykły	*ordinary, usual*	mam alergię na	*I'm allergic to*

1 Find the word that means:

a check
b pay
c server

2 Is this correct? Answer Yes or No.

a **Kobieta** means *server.*
b The word for *stamp* is **zwykły**.
c Take a **gościem** means take a *table.*

Conversations

06.02 *The following day Maria and Andrew meet in a café in Market Square in the heart of Kraków's Old Town.*

1 What do Maria and Andrew order?

Kelnerka	Dzień dobry. Słucham państwa?
Maria	Poproszę kawę i sernik.
Andrew	A ja poproszę herbatę i lody kawowe.
Kelnerka	Proszę bardzo.

06.03 *Later . . .*

2 What does Maria ask the server?

Maria	Poproszę rachunek.
Kelnerka	Proszę.
Andrew	Chciałbym zapłacić rachunek.
Maria	Wykluczone. Jesteś moim gościem.
Andrew	Dziękuję bardzo.

3 Read the conversations then answer true or false.

- **a** Andrew orders ice cream.
- **b** Maria orders tea and cheesecake.
- **c** Andrew does not want to pay the check.
- **d** **Wykluczone** means *I'd love to.*

Language discovery

1 Can you figure out the English for these foods?

- **a** hamburger
- **b** ser
- **c** mleko
- **d** wódka
- **e** tort
- **f** woda mineralna
- **g** zupa pomidorowa
- **h** jogurt
- **i** czekolada

2 Did you notice the gender of the nouns?

1 WHAT TO ORDER

Look at the **dania** (*dishes*) on the menu.

MENU

Przystawki
Zupy
Dania bezmięsne
Dania wegetariańskie
Desery
Alkohole

2 ASKING POLITELY

Poproszę (or simply **proszę**) is used when you would like to ask for something politely. Literally, it means *I'll ask for*. In practice it means *Can I have ... please?*

3 SAYING IT CORRECTLY

How do you use **poproszę** correctly? **Poproszę**, just like **mam** (*I have*), is followed by the direct object (*Can I have . . . what?*).

Masculine nouns and neuter nouns referring to inanimate things don't change their basic form.

To jest rachunek.	**Poproszę rachunek.**
This is the check.	*Can I have the check, please?*

Feminine nouns ending in **-a** change the **-a** to **-ę**.

To jest kanapka.
This is a sandwich.

Poproszę kanapkę.
Can I have a sandwich, please?

To jest herbata.
This is tea.

Poproszę herbatę.
Can I have (some) tea, please?

Practice

1 **Complete each sentence in Polish.**
  a To jest bilet. Poproszę ________.
  b To jest rachunek. Poproszę ________.
  c To jest zupa. Poproszę ________.

2 **Do you agree? Answer Yes or No.**
  a I'll say **To jest ciasto** to order a cake.
  b My friend will say **Poproszę kanapkę** to order a sandwich.
  c **Poproszę kawę** means *This is coffee.*

3 **Answer true or false.**
  a *Tea* is a masculine noun in Polish.
  b **To jest piwo** means that you'd like a beer.
  c **Herbata** changes to **herbatek** with **proproszę**.

4 **Which headings on a menu do these foods belong to? Choose a word from the box.**

Desery Zupy Dania mięsne Dania Wegetariańskie Alkohole

  a sznycel
  b barszcz
  c lody
  d rosół
  e sernik
  f pomidory
  g wino

5 **Order items using the menu from Exercise 4 and pay the check.**
  a Poproszę ________.
  b Poproszę ________ *(cheesecake)*.
  c Poproszę ________ *(any kind of soup)*.
  d Poproszę ________ *(wine)*.

Pronunciation

06.04 **Listen to the audio.** What gives Polish its distinctive sound and fearsome reputation? The sets of consonants without a vowel. Don't be frightened! When we *say Is there any fresh cheese?* we produce combinations in English much like Polish [szcz] and [ść], and when we *say It's time to close shop* we produce a combination like the [psz] at the beginning of **Przepraszam.**

Look at these common consonant combinations. Spelling is between < > and pronunciation using Polish spelling is between [ ].

<prz> or <psz>	[p-sz]*	as in **przepraszam** (*excuse me*)
<krz> or <ksz>	[k-sz]	as in **krzyczeć** (*shout*), **większy** (*bigger*)
<trz> or <tsz>	[t-sz]	as in **trzeba** (*you need to*), **trzy** (*three*)
<szcz>	[sz-cz]	as in **deszcz** (*rain*)
<żdż>	[ż-dż]	as in **drożdżówka** (*teacake*), **przyjeżdżać** (*arrive*)
<chrz> or <ch-sz>	[ch-sz]	as in **chrzan** (*horseradish*), **chrześcijański** (*Christian*)
<skrz>	[s-k-sz]	as in **skrzypce** (*violin*)
<sch>	[s-ch]	as in **schody** (*stairs*), **wyschnąć** (*to dry*)
<tch>	[t-ch]	as in **tchórz** (*coward*), **natchnienie** (*inspiration*)
<ść> or <źdź>	[ś-ć]	as in **kość** (*bone*), **dość** (*enough*), **gwóźdź** (*nail*)
<źdź>	[ź-dź]	as in **źdźbło** (*blade of grass*), **jeździć** (*to go*)

1 Listen to the audio again and give the following words in Polish.

a rain
b stairs
c nail
d three
e violin
f enough
g bone
h horseradish
i excuse me

2 Find an example of a word with these sounds.

a [sz-cz]
b [ś-ć]
c [k-sz]

You may be puzzled why the **prz** combination is pronunced [psz] and not [pż] – it's all to do with the process called de-voicing, explained in Unit 7.

Listen and understand

1 06.05 **Listen to the conversation.**

Andrew	Poproszę tę widokówkę.
Kobieta	Proszę.
Andrew	Ile płacę?
Kobieta	Dwa pięćdziesiąt.

2 What does Andrew want to do?

a buy a notebook **b** buy a stamp **c** buy a postcard

3 How much does he pay?

a 5 złotych 20 groszy **b** 2 złote 50 groszy **c** 4 złote 20 groszy

The Polish currency złoty changes form depending on the amount:

1 złoty
2–4 złote
5–21 złotych

After 21, the form should be chosen using the rule above, but based only on the final digit. For example:

24 złote (the final digit – 4 – takes the form złote)

58 złotych (the final digit – 8 – takes the form złotych)

4 Listen to the conversation again and complete the missing words.

a Poproszę tę ________? ________.
b Ile ________? ________ pięćdziesiąt.

AT THE KIOSK

Andrew is at a newsagent's kiosk where you can usually buy many small items.

Look at other items you can buy at the kiosk.

gazeta	**notatnik**
czasopismo	**słodycze**
bilet autobusowy	**tabletki**

5 **How would Andrew ask the kobieta politely to:**
   - **a** buy a magazine?
   - **b** buy a notebook?
   - **c** buy a newspaper?

Reading, writing and speaking

1 **Read the conversation.**

Sprzedawca	Słucham?
Andrew	Poproszę znaczek do Wielkiej Brytanii.
Sprzedawca	Zwykły czy priorytetowy?
Andrew	Poproszę priorytetowy.

2 **Answer the questions.**
   - **a** Andrew is at a (café/news stand/post office).
   - **b** The **sprzedawca** is a (server/newsagent/postal assistant).
   - **c** Andrew wants to buy a (stamp/map/postcard).

3 **Complete the conversation.**

Sprzedawca	Słucham?
You	________
Sprzedawca	________
You	________

4 **06.06 Listen to the conversation from Exercise 1 and try to imitate the speakers. Now, say your own conversation from Exercise 3 out loud and check your pronunciation.**

Sprzedawca	Słucham?
Andrew	Poproszę znaczek do Wielkiej Brytanii.
Sprzedawca	Zwykły czy priorytetowy?
Andrew	Poproszę priorytetowy.

Andrew asked for **znaczek priorytetowy** (as opposed to **zwykły**). Another type of **list** (*letter*) in Poland is **list polecony** (*sent by registered mail*).

Go further

BEING OFFICIAL

Asking for something politely using **poproszę** is very common. But there is another, less polite but more official way of asking for something. This type is usually used by an official such as a ticket inspector who may say:

Bilet proszę (*ticket please*) instead of **Poproszę bilet** (*can I have a ticket please?*).

BEING EXTRA POLITE

On the other hand, if you want to be extra polite you can say **Czy mogę prosić o . . .** (*Can I ask for . . . ?*). The good news is that the spelling of the noun you are asking for does not change from one form to another.

1 Look at the table and compare how these forms are used.

bilet	**Poproszę bilet.**	**Bilet proszę.**	**Czy mogę prosić o bilet?**
kawa	**Poprosze kawę.**	**Kawę proszę.**	**Czy mogę prosić o kawę?**
piwo	**Poproszę piwo.**	**Piwo proszę.**	**Czy mogę prosić o piwo?**
dokumenty	**Poproszę dokumenty.**	**Dokumenty proszę.**	(a)
sok	**Poproszę sok.**	(b)	(c)
herbata	(d)	(e)	(f)
reklamówka	(g)	(h)	(i)
znaczek	(j)	(k)	(l)
rachunek	(m)	(n)	(o)

2 Complete the missing forms in the table.

Test yourself

1 Say the sentences in Polish.

- **a** Can I have a coffee, please?
- **b** Can I have (a piece of) cheesecake, please?
- **c** I'd like to pay the check, please.
- **d** Out of the question. You are my guest.
- **e** Can I have an first class stamp for Great Britain, please?
- **f** I'm vegetarian (man).
- **g** I'm allergic to nuts.

2 Translate more sentences into Polish.

- **a** Can I have a tea, please?
- **b** Can I have a coffee, please?
- **c** Can I have a stamp, please?
- **d** Can I have a guidebook, please?
- **e** I'd like some tea, please.
- **f** I'd like some coffee, please.
- **g** I'd like to buy a stamp.
- **h** I'd like to buy a guidebook.

3 What's wrong with the sentences?

- **a** Barbara jest emerytem.
- **b** Andrew jest Polką.
- **c** Poproszę kawa.
- **d** Chciałbym zamówić znaczek.
- **e** Jestem dwadzieścia lat.
- **f** Mam ochotę na herbata.
- **g** Musi pan koniecznie kupić Wawel.

4 06.07 Respond in Polish to the questions and statements. Listen to the audio to check your answers and practice pronunciation.

	QUESTIONS/STATEMENTS	YOUR RESPONSE
a	**Poproszę rachunek.**	*Here you are.*
b	**Słucham panią/pana?**	*Can I have a coffee, please?*
c	**Chciał(a)bym zapłacić rachunek.**	*Out of the question. You are my guest.*
d	**Ile płacę?**	*Two złote and fifty groszy.*

SELF CHECK

I CAN...
... ask for things politely.
... order food.
... ask for and pay the check.
... buy stamps and postcards.
... say I'm hungry and tired.

Review 2

1 Translate the following into English.

a Co pan musi zrobić?
b Muszę wrócić do domu.
c Musimy się spotkać.
d Musimy.
e Muszę zobaczyć Warszawę.
f Nie, nie musi pan.
g Chcę się napić kawy.
h Koniecznie?

2 Choose the correct word to complete each sentence.

a musi/musicie — Dlaczego ______ pani iść?
b muszę/muszą — Oni ______ zjeść obiad.
c musisz/muszą — (Ty) nie ______ się od razu (*immediately*) rozpakować.
d muszę/musimy — A my ______ koniecznie zadzwonić do domu.
e pan/panowie — Czy ______ musi już jechać?
f spotkać/zwiedzić — Musimy się ______ znowu.
g spotkać/zwiedzić — Muszą państwo ______ Wrocław.

3 Przepraszam (*Sorry*) literally means *I apologize*. Say the following in Polish.

a He apologizes.
b They're apologizing.
c We're apologizing.
d Why doesn't she apologize?

4 Choose the correct preposition to complete each sentence.

a na/w/do/z/za — Jestem ______ emeryturze.
b na/w/do/zz/a — Idę ______ domu.
c na/w/do/z/za — Siedzi ______ domu.
d na/w/do/z/za — Dziękuję ______ wszystko.
e na/w/do/z/za — Chcemy zamówić stolik ______ restauracji.
f Na/W/Do/Z/Za — ______ którą godzinę?
g Na/W/Do/Z/Za — ______ widzenia.
h Na/W/Do/Z/Za — ______ zobaczenia.
i na/w/do/z/za — Chciałbym się spotkać ______ tobą.
j na/w/do/z/za — Chcielibyśmy zjeść kolację ______ hotelu.

5 Complete the sentences with a word from the box.

przewodnika	zrobić	czekają	zwiedzić	zamówić	pomocy

a Nasze (*our*) dzieci chciałyby ________ Poznań.
b Chciałabyś ________ zakupy?
c Potrzebujemy ________ .
d Chciałybyśmy ________ taksówkę.
e Czekamy na ________ .
f Państwo ________ na autobus?

6 Read the conversational snippets. Put them in an order that makes sense.

a Proszę bardzo.
b A ja poproszę wodę mineralną.
c Poproszę sernik i lody.
d Słucham panie?
e Dzień dobry paniom.

7 Are the following statements true or false?

a **Jem obiad.** means *I'm eating breakfast.*
b **Jemy bigos.** means *We are eating hunters' stew.*
c **Chciałby zobaczyć Londyn.** means *I would like to see London.*
d **Chciałaby pani pójść na obiad?** means *Would you like to go for dinner, madam?*
e **Nie mam ochoty na herbatę.** means *I don't like tea.*
f **Czy ta aktorka jest dobra?** means *Is this actress good?*
g **Lubię kuchnię wegańską.** means *I like vegetarian cuisine.*

8 Look at the answers. What are the questions?

a Film zaczyna się o szóstej.
b Jest (godzina) czwarta.
c Na dziewiątą.
d Chciałbym przyjść o pierwszej.
e Muszę wyjśc o dziesiątej.

9 Make sentences. Match the beginnings with the endings.

a Chciałbym kupić . . .
b Jestem . . .
c Mam . . .
d Musimy . . .

1 czas i pieniądze.
2 widokówki.
3 spotkać się jutro.
4 z Anglii.

10 Complete the conversation.

Andrew	Dziękuję za ________ .
Maria	Nie ma za co.
Andrew	Tak bardzo ________ znaleźć moją rodzinę.
Maria	Oczywiście, ________ . Do ________ jutro.

11 Answer the questions in Polish.

a Czy jesteś detektywem czy architektem?
b Czy Toffik to zły pies?
c Czy chciałabyś zwiedzić Muzeum Narodowe czy Wawel?
d Ile masz lat?

12 Look at this advert in a local paper. What is on offer?

Ogłoszenie
Masz czas? Lubisz dzieci? Mamy oferty pracy.
Prosimy o kontakt: www.nianie.pl

13 Look at the business listings and answer the following questions.

Salon antyków
Ewa Brzezińska
Ekspert – sztuka renesansowa i barokowa
ul. Królewska 34
00-245 Warszawa
Tel: salon – 22 234 67 89
Tel komórkowy – 685 276 140

Dentysta
Marek Wierzbicki
Jesteś nerwowym pacjentem?
Zamów wizytę dzisiaj.
ul. Floriańska 10
31-021 Kraków
tel: 635 345 996

Natalia Wilkowska
Architekt
Nowe projekty
Renowacja starych domów
ul. Krucza 3
00-568 Warszawa
Tel kom: 645 335 875

a Who can design your house?
b Can Natalia assist in a renovation of an old house?
c What does Ewa specialize in?
d Who is especially welcome at Marek's practice?

14 What's wrong with these sentences?

a Tomasz Krajewska jest lekarzem.
b Ewa masz psa.
c Ona chciałby studiować medycynę.
d Maria muszę już iść.

15 Look at the list of verbs. Match the verbs with the nouns in the box.

muzeum herbaty informacji zdjęcie pomocy dokumenty prezent

a zasięgnąć
b potrzebować
c znaleźć
d kupić
e zwiedzić
f zrobić
g napić się

7

In this unit you will learn how to:

- » express likes and dislikes.
- » express preferences.
- » talk about food and cuisines.
- » find simple information on menus.

Lubię kuchnię polską

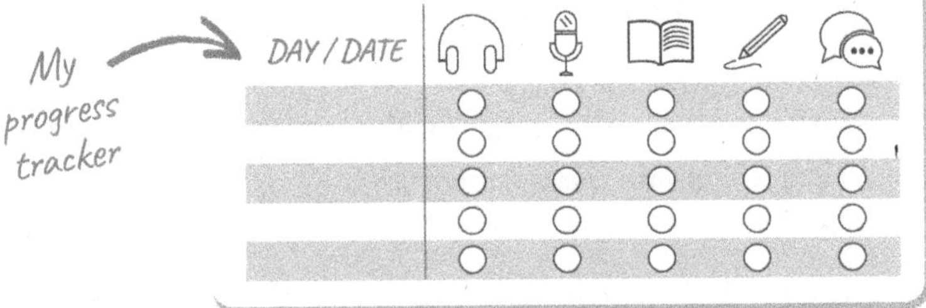

What, where and when to eat

Most Polish people start their day early with **śniadanie** (*breakfast*) followed by **drugie śniadanie** (lit. *a second breakfast*), a 15–20 minute break for a **kanapka** (*sandwich*) around 10:30–11:00. Although **przerwa obiadowa** (*lunch break*) can be between 12:00–14:00, **obiad** (*dinner*) is usually eaten around 16:00–18:00. The word **lunch** (pronounced as in English) is also increasingly popular. The last meal of the day is **kolacja** (*supper*) eaten between 19:00–21:00. Home is still the most traditional place to eat, but eating out is something many Polish people enjoy.

Poland has a strong tradition of **kawiarnie** – in the past, these were frequented by artists, writers and political activists, and today some of them still opt for a more vintage decor. If you are traveling, **zajazd** (*a travelers inn*) is a traditional stop for refreshments and a place to sleep. **Bar mleczny** – a place to eat inexpensive, home-cooked dishes – are frequented today by students, pensioners and savvy tourists.

What meal would you eat at 11:00?

a śniadanie
b kolacja
c kanapka

Vocabulary builder

07.01 Listen as you look at the words and complete the translations. Then listen again and try to imitate the speakers.

MORE BORROWED WORDS

Galeria	___
Muzeum	___

ABOUT ART

obrazy (obraz)	*paintings*
słynny	___
chodźmy (chodzić > pochodzić)	*let's* ___
zobaczyć (widzieć > zobaczyć)	*see*

WORDS YOU MAY REMEMBER

głodny	___
piwo	___
sernik	___

NEW EXPRESSIONS

trochę	*a bit*
obiad	*lunch, dinner*
kuchnia	*kitchen, cooking, cuisine, food*
bigos	*traditional Polish cabbage stew called 'hunters' stew'*
rynek	*market*
Sukiennice	*the Cloth Hall*
narodowe (narodowy)	*national*
pytać o [+ acc.] (pytać > zapytać)	*ask about*
dlaczego	*why*
chętnie (chętny)	*willingly, with pleasure*

1 What do you think?

- **a** Does **słynny** mean *famous* or *fake*?
- **b** Is the word for *why* **rynek**?
- **c** Can you buy clothes at **Sukiennice**?
- **d** Does **Jestem trochę głodny** mean *I'd like a little cheescake*?

Conversations

07.02 *Andrew and Maria have spent the morning in the archives. Maria suggests going for lunch.*

1 What does Andrew like to eat?

Andrew	Jestem trochę głodny.
Maria	Chodźmy na obiad. Czy lubi pan kuchnię polską?
Andrew	Tak, lubię bigos, sernik i polskie piwo.

07.03 *A five-minute walk away they find the Pod Aniołami restaurant and go in.*

2 What are Maria and Andrew talking about now?

Maria	Co chciałby pan zobaczyć w Krakowie?
Andrew	Chciałbym zobaczyć Rynek, Sukiennice, Wawel i Muzeum Narodowe.

3 Read the conversations and answer the questions.

a How does Andrew say he is hungry?
b If you order **bigos**, what sort of dish will you eat?
c What else does Andrew like to eat in Poland?
d Which places would Andrew like to visit in Kraków?

4 Complete the conversations with a Polish expression.

a
You What Polish foods do you like?
Andrew ______________. It's a tasty stew.

b
Andrew What do you want to see next?
You ______________ Wawel i Museum Narodowe.

5 Choose the words that go together.

a	obiad	dlaczego	kuchnia
b	rynek	galeria	chętnie

Language discovery

1 Look at the different types of cuisine.

Types of cuisine	I like . . . cuisine	Example
kuchnia polska	*Polish*	**Lubię kuchnię polską.**
kuchnia indyjska	*Indian*	**Lubię kuchnię indyjską.**
kuchnia chińska	*Chinese*	**Lubię kuchnię chińską.**
kuchnia włoska	*Italian*	**Lubię kuchnię włoską.**
kuchnia francuska	*French*	**Lubię kuchnię** __________.
kuchnia meksykańska	*Mexican*	**Lubię kuchnię** __________.
kuchnia hiszpańska	*Spanish*	**Lubię kuchnię** __________.
kuchnia tajwańska	*Taiwanese*	**Lubię kuchnię** __________.
kuchnia tajska	*Thai*	**Lubię kuchnię** __________.
kuchnia grecka	*Greek*	**Lubię kuchnię** __________.

2 Try to figure out the remaining forms and complete the table.

DESCRIBING IT

The expression **kuchnia polska** illustrates an important principle in Polish related to the order in which adjectives and nouns can appear. In Polish, just as in English, nouns can follow adjectives:

zły pies *vicious dog*

ciekawa książka *an interesting book*

But if the noun represents one person, place, or thing among others of the same group, the order will be reversed and the noun will precede its adjective.

07.04 **Here are examples that illustrate the point. Listen and repeat.**

gabinet okulistyczny	*optician's*
gabinet dentystyczny	*dentist's*
gabinet kosmetyczny	*beauty salon*
aparat słuchowy	*hearing aid*
aparat fotograficzny	*camera*
język polski	*Polish language*
język angielski	*English language*
salon fryzjerski	*hairdresser's*
salon samochodowy	*car showroom*
straż miejska	*town guard*
straż pożarna	*fire brigade*
straż więzienna	*prison guard*
dworzec kolejowy	*railway station*
dworzec autobusowy	*bus/coach station*

Practice

1 Cover the list above. Listen again and choose the word you hear.

a dworzec (kolejowy/fryzjerski) (*railway station*)

b straż (polski/pożarna) (*fire brigade*)

c aparat (kosmetyczny/słuchowy) (*hearing aid*)

2 Choose the correct answer.

a A **gabinet kosmetyczny** is a (beauty salon/dentist/optician).

b An **aparat** is probably a (camera/mechanical device).

c (**Miejska/Język**) is the word for language.

d A *hairdresser's* is a (**salon fryzjerski/salon samochodowy**).

3 Put the name of the cuisine in Polish.

a ginger, almonds, sweet and sour chicken

b fettucine, tomato sauce, linguine

c curry, ginger, tandoori

d sausage and hunters' stew

e burritos and tamales

Pronunciation: *w* and *rz*

1 07.05 Listen and repeat.

w	tw [tf]	**twarz** (*face*), **twój** (*your*), **twardy** (*hard*)
	kw [kf]	**kwadrat** (*square*), **kwartał** (*quarter of the year*), **kwarc** (*quartz*)
	sw [sf]	**swój** (*one's own*), **swoboda** (*freedom*), **Swarzędz** [sfażenc] (*Polish town*)
rz	prz [psz]	**przepraszam** (*excuse me*), **przykry** (*unpleasant*), **przyloty** (*arrivals*)
	trz [tsz]	**trzeba** (*you need to*), **trzaskać** (*slam*), **trząść** (*shake*)
	chrz [chsz]	**chrząszcz** (*beetle*), **chrzan** (*horseradish*), **chrząkać** (*to clear one's throat*)
	krz [ksz]	**krzesło** (*chair*), **krzak** (*shrub*), **krzyczeć** (*shout*)
	wsz [fsz]	**wszystko** (*everything*), **wszelki** (*every*), **wszy** (*flees*)

2 Look at the table again.

a What does **w** sound like? [w]/[t]/[f]

b What does **rz** sound like? [rz]/[sz]/[z]

3 Look at the following words. What consonants come before w and rz? Say your answers out loud in Polish.

a t**w**arz

b k**w**artał

c s**w**oboda

d p**rz**ykry

e ch**rz**an

f k**rz**ak

4 Go through the table and say the words out loud as you go along.

5 Now cover the table, listen again, and give the Polish words.

a you need to

b face

c arrivals

d everything

e horseradish

f excuse me

Conversation

07.06 *Maria's keen to find out about Andrew's taste in art.*

1 For what special reason does Maria ask Andrew about Leonardo da Vinci?

Maria	Czy lubi pan obrazy Leonarda da Vinci?
Andrew	Tak, bardzo. Dlaczego pani pyta?
Maria	W Krakowie jest słynny obraz Leonarda *Dama z łasiczką*. Czy chciałby pan go zobaczyć?
Andrew	Bardzo chętnie. Lubię zwiedzać galerie i muzea.

2 Now read the conversation and answer the questions.

a What title does Maria give Leonardo's painting?
b Does Andrew like Leonardo's paintings?
c What else does he like visiting besides galleries?
d Does **Bardzo chętnie** mean *I'd love to*?

> TIP
> Maria mistakes the name of Leonardo's famous painting. The correct title is **'Dama z gronostajem'** (*Lady with an Ermine*). Whatever the name, the painting is well worth seeing.

3 Find the Polish expression in the dialogue for the following.

a Yes, very much so.
b a famous painting
c Do you like...?

4 Now read the conversation again and say it out loud as you go along.

Language discovery

USING *I LIKE* . . .

As in English, you can use *like* with a noun as a direct object or with an *-ing* form of a verb.

1 Look at the table.

Person: 1st, 2nd, 3rd Singular and plural	With direct object With -ing verb	English translation
ja lubię	**Lubię galerie.** **Lubię zwiedzać galerie.**	*I like galleries.* *I like visiting galleries.*
ty lubisz	**Lubisz galerie.** **Lubisz zwiedzać galerie.**	*You like galleries.* *You like visiting galleries.*
on lubi/ona lubi/ono lubi	**On/ona/ono lubi galerie.** **On/ona/ono lubi zwiedzać galerie.**	*S/he/it likes galleries.* *S/he/it likes visiting galleries.*
pan/pani lubi	**Pan/pani lubi galerie.** **Pan/pani lubi zwiedzać galerie.**	*Sir/madam likes galleries.* *Sir/madam likes visiting galleries.*
my lubimy	**Lubimy galerie.** **Lubimy zwiedzać galerie.**	*We like galleries.* *We like visiting galleries.*
wy lubicie	**Lubicie galerie.** **Lubicie zwiedzać galerie.**	*You like galleries.* *You like visiting galleries.*
oni lubią **one lubią**	**Oni/one lubią galerie.** **Oni/one lubią zwiedzać galerie.**	*They like galleries.* *They like visiting galleries.*
panowie/panie lubią **państwo**	**Panowie/panie lubią galerie.** **Państwo lubią galerie.** **Panowie/panie lubią zwiedzać galerie.**	*Gentlemen/ladies like galleries.* *Ladies and gentlemen like galleries.* *Gentlemen/ladies like visiting galleries.*

Do you agree? Answer Yes or No.

- **a** Use **zwiedzać** with the *-ing* form a verb.
- **b** Use **ty lubisz** to say *we like*.
- **c** *You like galleries* is **Lubimy galerie**.

You can also use *like* with an infinitive (*I like to leave at 3:00*): **Lubię kawę** and **Lubię pić kawę**. The form **pić** is an infinitive – the basic dictionary form of the verb.

Go further

VOICED AND VOICELESS CONSONANTS

Polish consonants can also be divided into voiced or voiceless consonants.

Voiced consonants	**b, d, g, w, z, ż, rz, dż, dź** **l**	vibrate vocal chords except l, all have **voiceless counterparts**
Voiceless consonants	**p, t, k, f, s, sz, sz, cz, ć**	do not vibrate vocal chords use same shape of the mouth are counterparts of voiced consonants are more powerful can **de-voice**
NOTES: Pronounce **w** and **rz** as [f] and [sz] after a voiceless consonant. Two-letter combinations equal one sound and one consonant.		

DE-VOICING

De-voicing is the process of a voiced consonant turning into a voiceless one. De-voicing is very common in Polish. Words ending in a voiced consonant (**b**, **d**, **z**, **w**, **g**, etc.) are pronounced with the voiceless counterpart: **ogród** (*garden*) > [ogrut]

1 07.07 **Listen and repeat.**

lew	*lion*	[lef]
chleb	*bread*	[chlep]
grzyb	*mushroom*	[gżyp]
obiad	*dinner*	[obiat]
dąb	*oak*	[domp]
paw	*peacock*	[paf]
twarz	*face*	[tfasz]

2 Insert the voiceless counterpart: b ________ **d** ________ **g** ________ **ż** ________ **rz** ________ **dż** ________

3 Read the words in Exercise 1 and give the Polish words and pronunciation for the following.

a mushroom

b oak

c lion

d face

Test yourself

1 Say the sentences in Polish.

a Do you like Polish cuisine?
b What would you like to see in Kraków?
c I'd like to see the Market Square and the Cloth Hall.
d I like Chinese cuisine but I don't like Indian cuisine.

2 Complete the sentences.

a Lubię ________ polskie piwo.
b Czy lubi pani pić gorącą ________ ?
c Maria lubi ________ muzyki klasycznej.
d Lubię ________ filmy Kieślowskiego.

3 Match the verbs and nouns.

1 słuchać	**8** mieć	**a** informacji	**h** owoce
2 tańczyć	**9** mieszkać	**b** galerię	**i** psa
3 jeść	**10** mówić	**c** tango	**j** herbatę
4 pić	**11** zamówić	**d** widokówkę	**k** w Krakowie
5 oglądać	**12** zasięgnąć	**e** muzyki	**l** film
6 zwiedzać	**13** kupić	**f** stolik	**m** Rynek
7 zobaczyć		**g** po polsku	

4 07.08 **Respond in Polish to the questions. Listen to the recording to check your answers and practice pronunciation.**

	QUESTION	YOUR RESPONSE
a	**Czy lubisz obrazy Leonarda?**	*Yes, I do (like).*
b	**Jaką kuchnię lubisz?**	*I like Polish and Italian cuisine.*

SELF CHECK

	I CAN. . .
●	. . . express likes and dislikes.
●	. . . express preferences.
●	. . . talk about food and cuisines.

8

In this unit you will learn how to:

» ask for permission.
» say what needs to be done.
» say what is and is not allowed.
» say what is worth doing.
» understand and give simple directions.

Czy można zapłacić kartą?

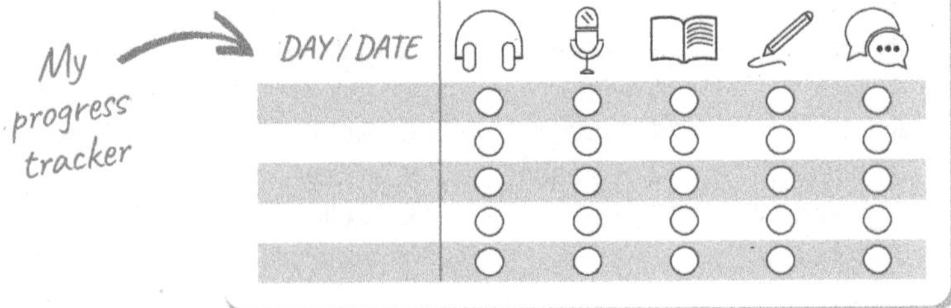

Discovering mysteries in Poland

Unlikely as it may seem, Poland has enough **tajemnice** (*mysteries*) around Teutonic knights, amber and works of art to fill the pages of many a **dreszczowiec** (*thriller*).

Gdańsk's proximity gave the Teutonic Knights control over the **bursztyn** (*amber*) trade, and today you can see an impressive collection in their extraordinary **zamek** (*castle*) at Malbork. Some say that a fabulous amber **skarb** (*treasure*) hidden by the Knights still awaits discovery. A second mystery surrounds art. In the course of its turbulent history, Poland has been robbed of its most valuable **dzieła sztuki** (*pieces of art*). One of the great mysteries is the disappearance of the painting by Raphael, *Portrait of a Young Man*, looted by Nazis from the Czartoryski Museum in Kraków. Despite the intensive search for the painting, its whereabouts remain unknown.

What does the book title *Tajemnica bursztynowego skarbu* mean?

Vocabulary builder

08.01 Listen as you look at the words and complete the translations. Then listen again and try to imitate the speakers.

SHOPPING AT A MUSEUM SHOP

magnes	________
album	________
przewodnik	________
plakat	________
zakładka	________
karta kredytowa	________
pocztówka	________
książka	________

NEW EXPRESSIONS

wolno	*it's allowed, one may*
robić zdjęcia robić > zrobić; zdjęcie	*take photographs*
przykro mi (przykry, ja)	*I'm sorry.*
szkoda	*pity, shame*
gdzie	*where*
w	*in*
jeszcze	*still, besides, another*
można	*it's possible to*
itd. (i tak dalej)	*etc.*
kupić (kupować > kupić)	*buy*
nie wiem (wiedzieć)	*I don't know.*
trzeba	*one needs to/you need to*
zapytać (pytać > zapytać)	*ask*
warto	*worth*
zapłacić za + acc. (płacić > zapłacić)	*pay for*

What is the correct Polish for the following expressions?

a it's allowed (**można/wolno**)

b you need to (**trzeba/gdzie**)

c I'm sorry (**jeszcze/przykro mi**)

Conversation

08.02 *Maria takes Andrew to the Muzeum Czartoryskich.*

1 What does Andrew want to do?

Andrew	Czy wolno robić zdjęcia w muzeum?
Maria	Nie, nie wolno. Przykro mi.
Andrew	Szkoda. Gdzie można kupić przewodnik?
Maria	W sklepie muzealnym.
Andrew	Co jeszcze można tam kupić?
Maria	Książki, albumy, plakaty, zakładki, magnesy, pocztówki, itd.
Andrew	A czy można kupić znaczki?
Maria	Nie wiem. Trzeba zapytać.

2 Now read the conversation and answer the questions.

a What does **szkoda** mean?

b What is Andrew interested in buying?

c Where does Maria say he can buy this?

3 If you ask for książka you get (a book/postcards/a coffee table book).

Language discovery

Predict the correct grammar.

- **a** How do you say *it is all right to take photographs?* (**Warto zobaczyć/Można robić zdjęcia**)
- **b** What is the plural of *paintings*? (**obraze/obrazy**)
- **c** How do you ask for a calendar? For calendars? (**kalendarz/ kalendarze; kalendarze/kalendarzy**)
- **d** How do you tell someone *You can go in*? (**Wolno wejść/Warto zobaczyć**)

1 CAN, NEED, ALLOWED, IT'S WORTH

Można, trzeba, wolno, warto – *one can, one needs to, it's allowed, it's worth*. These are words you will hear a lot in Polish. We've grouped them here not just because you can use them in similar situations, but also because they are relatively easy to apply in everyday conversations. Polish people often use them because they are a neat way of avoiding addressing the person you are speaking to.

Można, trzeba, wolno and **warto** are always followed by a verb in its basic (infinitive) form:

Można robić zdjęcia.	*One can take photographs.*
Trzeba pojechać autobusem.	*You need to go by bus.*
Wolno wejść.	*You can go/come in.*
Warto zobaczyć katedrę.	*It's worth seeing the cathedral.*

Nie wolno! is what you will often hear parents saying to their children when they want to tell them off.

2 CREATING PLURALS

How to create plural forms for masculine nouns? You can do it in a number of ways.

▶ Add **-y** to a noun in the basic, singular form.

Singular form	English	Plural form
album	*coffee table book*	**albumy**
plakat	*poster*	**plakaty**
magnes	*magnet*	**magnesy**
obraz	*painting*	**obrazy**

▶ If a singular form ends in **-k** in Polish, for historical reasons **-k** cannot be followed by **-y** and must be replaced by **-i**.

przewodnik	*guide(book)*	**przewodniki**

▶ When a noun ends in **-rz**, **-l** or **-j**, add **-e** to the basic form.

kalendarz	*calendar*	**kalendarze**

▶ Some masculine nouns lose the **-e** from the ending **-ek**.

znaczek	*stamp*	**znaczki**

Practice

1 Choose the correct word. There may be more than one option.

- **a** Można/Trzeba/Wolno/Warto zwiedzić Kraków.
- **b** Można/Trzeba/Wolno/Warto tu palić (*smoke here*).
- **c** Można/Trzeba/Wolno/Warto zobaczyć 'Damę z łasiczką'.

2 Create the Polish plural forms.

- **a** dom (*house/home*)
- **b** kot (*cat*)
- **c** numer (*number*)
- **d** adres (*address*)
- **e** sernik (*cheesecake*)
- **f** hotel (*hotel*)
- **g** kraj (*country*)
- **h** rachunek (*check*)

3 Create more plural forms.

- **a** sok (*juice*)
- **b** krok (*step*)
- **c** talerz (*plate*)
- **d** worek (*sack*)
- **e** samolot (*plane*)

Pronunciation

08.03 A CONFUSING CONSONANT COMBINATION: *CK*

1 **Pronounce these English words:** *pack, track, muck.*

2 **Pronounce these Polish words.**

a Say the surnames.

Buczacki	**Buczacka**
Krasicki	**Krasicka**
Mędrzycki	**Mędrzycka**
Mościcki	**Mościcka**

b Say the adjectives.

niemiecki *(German)*

szlachecki *(of Polish gentry)*

karpacki *(Carpathian)*

3 **Did you notice? Answer true or false.**

a In English *ck* is pronounced as two sounds.

b In Polish **ck** is pronounced as two sounds.

c In Polish **ck** is often followed by **-i** or **-a**.

4 **Did you pronounce both c and k in the Polish names and adjectives? Read them again out loud and check your pronunciation.**

Conversations

08.04 Andrew is enquiring about the location of the museum shop.

1 Is the shop on the ground floor?

Andrew	Gdzie jest sklep? Czy trzeba wyjść z muzeum?
Maria	Nie, można przejść korytarzem do sklepu. Trzeba iść prosto, potem po schodach w dół. Sklep jest na parterze.
Andrew	Co jeszcze warto kupić w sklepie?

08.05 Andrew has bought several things at the shop.

2 How would he like to pay for his purchases?

Andrew	Przepraszam, czy można zapłacić kartą kredytową?
Sprzedawczyni	Tak, można.

3 Now read the conversations and answer Yes or No.

a You have to leave the museum to get to the shop.
b The shop is straight ahead and up the stairs.
c The shop is on the ground floor.
d You can pay by credit card.

4 Which word is the odd one out?

a prosto	nie wiem	w dół
b na parterze	można	w sklepie
c gdzie	kupić	przejść
d w	co	do

Language discovery

MONEY AND PAYMENT

1 Look at the examples of currency and related terms.

(Note: The Polish currency 1 złoty = 100 groszy)

Polish	English
gotówka	*cash*
reszta	*change*
bankomat	*cash machine*
karta zbliżeniowa	*contactless card*

2 Complete the sentences.

a Czy można zapłacić ________?
b Czy można zapłacić ________?
c Proszę, to jest ________.
d Przepraszam, gdzie jest ________?

3 What's in your portfel (*wallet*)?

English	Polish
cash	(a)
(b)	**reszta**
cash machine	(c)
contactless card	(d)
(e)	**karta kredytowa**

4 Take a guess – what is the English word for monety?

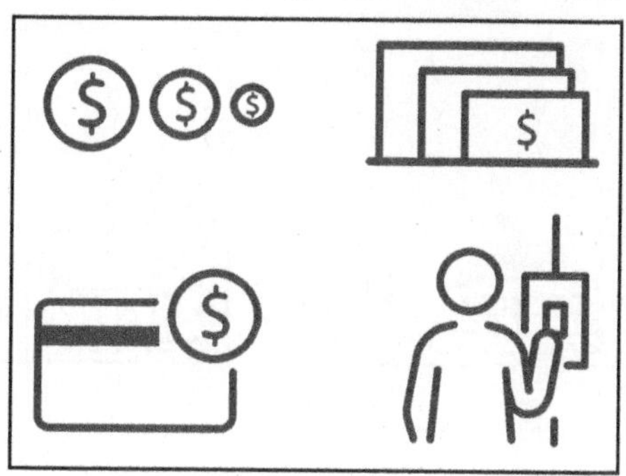

Go further

GETTING AROUND

1 Read the words that express directions.

z muzeum	*from/out of the museum*
przejść (przechodzić > przejść)	*go/come through, go/come across*
wyjść (wychodzić > wyjść)	*go out, come out*
korytarzem (korytarz)	*along the corridor*
do sklepu (sklep)	*to the shop*
prosto (prosty)	*straight*
po + locative	*after, along, by*
po schodach (schody)	*by the stairs*
w dół	*downwards*
na + locative	*(located) on, at*
na parterze (parter)	*on the ground floor (American first floor)*
w sklepie muzealnym (sklep, muzealny)	*in the museum shop*
windą (winda)	*in the lift*
podjazdem (dla osób niepełnosprawnych) (podjazd)	*down/up the ramp (for wheelchair users)*

2 Complete the missing words in the conversation.

Andrew Gdzie jest sklep? Czy trzeba ________ z muzeum?

Maria Nie, można przejść ________ ________. Trzeba iść ________, potem po schodach ________. Sklep jest ________.

Andrew Co jeszcze warto kupić ________?

3 Create your own conversation. Direct Maria to the museum shop.

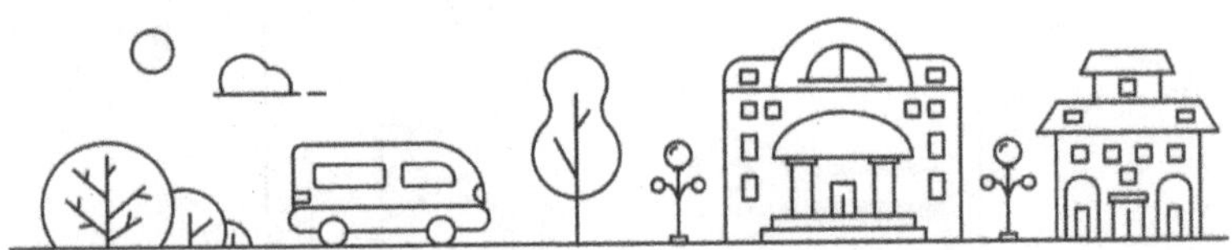

Test yourself

1 Give the plural forms of the following nouns.

a telefon
b komputer
c samochód

2 Say the sentences in Polish.

a Is taking photos allowed in the museum?
b I'm sorry, but it's not allowed.
c Pity.
d What else can you buy there?

3 08.06 **Respond in Polish to the questions and statements. Listen to the recording to check your answers and practice pronunciation.**

	QUESTIONS/STATEMENTS	YOUR RESPONSE
a	**Czy wolno robić zdjęcia w muzeum?**	*No, it's not allowed.*
b	**Gdzie jest sklep?**	*On the ground floor.*
c	**Gdzie można kupić przewodnik?**	*In the museum shop.*

4 Complete the sentences.

a Chciałbym ________ zdjęcia w galerii.
b Gdzie jest ________ muzealny?
c Czy mogę zapłacić ________ ________?

SELF CHECK

	I CAN...
●	... ask for permission.
●	... say what needs to be done.
●	... say what is and is not allowed.
●	... say what is worth doing.
●	... understand and give simple directions.

9

In this unit you will learn how to:

» ask questions.
» indicate time.
» arrange a meeting.
» describe a location.
» indicate frequency.

Wszystkiego najlepszego z okazji urodzin

My progress tracker

DAY / DATE					
	○	○	○	○	○
	○	○	○	○	○
	○	○	○	○	○
	○	○	○	○	○
	○	○	○	○	○

Celebrations

Polish people celebrate **urodziny** (*birthdays*) though some prefer to celebrate **imieniny** (*name days*), which are related to a patron saint. These are not religious celebrations, and are celebrated like birthdays — you still get a **prezent** (*present*) but nobody reminds you of your age. The Polish **kalendarz** (*calendar*) lists a couple of names under each day. Other traditional celebrations are related to **ślub** (*a wedding*) and **wesele** (*a wedding reception*), often organized at the **dom weselny** (*a wedding hall*). Despite the name, it may also be the venue for a **stypa** (*a wake*) after **pogrzeb** (*a funeral*). In fact, any party related to **rocznica** (*an anniversary*) can be organized there. Polish people like giving and receiving **kwiaty** (*flowers*) for celebrations regardless of gender.

When would you receive a card for your 25th wedding anniversary?

a dom weselny **b rocznica ślubu**

Vocabulary builder

09.01 **Listen as you look at the words and phrases and complete the English translations. Then listen again and try to imitate the speakers.**

ASKING AND ANSWERING QUESTIONS

co się stało (stawać się > stać się)	*what's ______*
co słychać	*how are ______?*
jaką (jaki)	______
dokąd	______ *(to)*
wytłumaczę (tłumaczyć > wytłumaczyć, ty)	*I'll ______ (it) to you.*
po drodze (po, droga)	______
niedaleko + gen.	______ *(from)*
tuż obok + gen.	______ *(to)*
obok Rynku	______ *to the Market Square*

NEW EXPRESSIONS

wszystko	*everything, all*
dla + genitive	*for, for the sake of*
dla ciebie (dla, ty)	*for you*
interesującą wiadomość (interesująca, wiadomość)	*an interesting piece of news*
w twoim hotelu (twój hotel)	*at/in your hotel*
chodźmy (chodzić > pochodzić)	*let's go*
jesteśmy umówieni (umówiony; umawiać się > umówić się)	*we've got an appointment/ we've arranged a meeting*
z Ewą (Ewa)	*with Ewa*
pracuje (pracować > popracować)	*she works*
do mojego biura (do, mój, biuro)	*to my office*
rozumiem (rozumieć > zrozumieć)	*I understand, I gather.*
szuka pan rodziny (szukać > poszukać, rodzina)	*you're looking for relatives/family*
moi przodkowie (mój, przodek)	*my ancestors*
pochodzą z + gen. (pochodzić)	*come, originate from*
mieszkali (mieszkać)	*lived*
byli (być)	*they were*
stary dwór	*old manor house*

Which phrase does NOT fit?

a chodźmy **b** jesteśmy umówieni **c** co słychać

Conversations

09.02 *Andrew is at his hotel when his phone rings.*

1 Why does Maria want to meet Andrew?

Andrew	Słucham.
Maria	Dzień dobry panie Andrzeju. Mówi Maria.
Andrew	Dzień dobry pani Mario. Co słychać?
Maria	Wszystko dobrze, dziękuję. Mam interesującą wiadomość dla pana. Kiedy możemy się spotkać?
Andrew	Dzisiaj?
Maria	Dobrze.
Andrew	Gdzie?
Maria	W pana hotelu.
Andrew	O której?
Maria	O czwartej.
Andrew	Dobrze. Do zobaczenia.
Maria	Do widzenia.

09.03 *Maria and Andrew meet.*

2 Why are they going to Market Square?

Andrew	Co się stało?
Maria	Mam fascynującą informację dla pana.
Andrew	Jaką informację?
Maria	Chodźmy. Wytłumaczę wszystko po drodze.
Andrew	Dokąd idziemy?
Maria	Niedaleko. Na ulicę Sienną. Tuż obok Rynku. Jesteśmy umówieni z Ewą.

3 Now read the conversations and answer true or false.

a Maria calls Andrew to invite him to a celebration.
b They meet at a florist's at 4:00.
c Maria is taking Andrew to Ewa's wedding.
d Maria has some interesting news for Andrew.

4 Find in the conversations the words that mean:

a What's happened? **b** Where **c** What time?

Language discovery

Read the answers. What are the questions?

a To jest poczta.

b To jest Julia.

c To jest pies.

d To jest w górach.

1 ASKING QUESTIONS: *WHAT, WHO, WHERE, WHEN*

Co (*what*), **kto** (*who*), **gdzie** (*where*) and **kiedy** (*when*) create open questions requiring more than a yes/no answer.

Co to jest?	*What is it?*
To jest poczta.	*It is a post office.*
Kto to jest?	*Who is it?*
To jest Karim.	*This is Karim.*
Gdzie to jest?	*Where is this?*
To jest w Krakowie.	*It is in Kraków.*
Kiedy to jest?	*When is it?*
To jest w piątek.	*It is on Friday.*

2 DESCRIBING LOCATION

1 Look at the table. Using gdzie (*what*) requires giving a location which usually means using a preposition (*in, at, on, above*, etc.).

In	**w Europie (Europa)** **w Warszawie (Warszawa)** **w Anglii (Anglia)** **w domu (dom)** **w sklepie (sklep)** **w hotelu (hotel)** **w pokoju (pokój)** but . . . **na ulicy (ulica)** **na placu (plac)**	*in Europe* *in Warsaw* *in England* *in the house* *in the shop* *in a hotel* *in a room* *in the street* *in the square*
At	**na uniwersytecie (uniwersytet)** **na dworcu (dworzec)**	*at the university* *at the station*
on/down/up	**na/po schodach (schody)**	*on/down/up the stairs*

2 Did you notice the change in spelling?

Prepositions of location

As you can see, both **w** and **na** are used to describe location.

Na is used with words such as **ulica**, **uniwersytet**, **dworzec**, **schody**, **plac**, as well as districts of towns.

na Starym Mieście	*in the Old Town*
na Mokotowie	*in Mokotów (a district of Warsaw)*

W or **we** is used with *house/home*, *shop*, *room* as well as with towns, villages and countries.

we Francji/Włoszech	*in France/Italy*
w Szkocji/Australii	*in Scotland/Australia*
w Londynie	*in London*

The best way to know when to use **w** or **na** is to learn the examples by heart.

> **TIP**
> Words like **archiwum** and **muzeum** do not change their spelling regardless of the context in which they are used.

3 DESCRIBING TIME

Look at the table. **Kiedy** (*when*) requires using words and expressions related to time.

a day	**dzisiaj** (or **dziś**) **wczoraj** **jutro**	*today* *yesterday* *tomorrow*
a time of day	**po południu** **wieczorem** **w nocy** **rano**	*in the afternoon* *in the evening* *at night* *in the morning*
frequency	**często** **czasami/czasem** **rzadko** **nigdy**	*often* *sometimes* *rarely* *never*

Practice

1 Yoko goes to Polish class in the evening. When does she go?

a dzisiaj
b po południu
c wieczorem
d rano

2 Order the times by frequency: 1 = most frequent.

a nigdy
b często
c czasami
d rzadko

3 Answer Yes or No.

a **Na placu** means *in the square.*
b **Po schodach** means *down/up the stairs.*
c **Na uniwersytecie** means *at the university.*

Pronunciation

1 09.04 **Listen and repeat.**

wy-sta-wa	*display*	**cy-try-na**	*lemon*
po-ma-rań-cza	*orange*	**her-ba-ta**	*tea*
ka-wiar-nia	*coffee shop*	**re-laks**	*relaxation*

2 Listen and repeat.

matematyka	[matemAtyka]	*mathematics*
fizyka	[fIzyka]	*physics*
gramatyka	[gramAtyka]	*grammar*
muzyka	[mUzyka]	*music*

biblioteka	[bibliOteka]	*library*
informatyka	[informAtyka]	*information technology*

3 Did you notice where the stress falls in the first group of words (Exercise 1)?

4 Did you notice where the stress falls in the second group of words (Exercise 2)?

TIP

Although the words in Exercise 2 should be pronounced this way, some people will in fact stress the second syllable from the end, which is a more modern way of pronouncing them.

Conversations

09.05 *Maria and Andrew walk along Floriańska Street to the Market Square to meet Ewa. By St Mary's Church they turn left into Sienna Street. Andrew is intrigued.*

1 Where does Ewa work?

Andrew	Kto to jest Ewa?
Maria	Ewa to moja przyjaciółka. Pracuje w Archiwum. Jest genealogiem.

TIP

When talking about professions, in most cases, it is correct to use either a masculine or a feminine form when talking about women. But although it is correct to say **Ewa jest genealogiem** and **Ewa jest genealożką**, the feminine form is becoming increasingly dominant.

09.06 *Ewa's already waiting for them in the foyer. Maria introduces them.*

2 What does Ewa know about Andrew?

Maria	Ewo, to jest pan Andrew Stewart.
Ewa	Dzień dobry panu.
Andrew	Bardzo mi miło.
Ewa	Chodźmy do mojego biura.
In Ewa's office . . .	
Ewa	Rozumiem, że szuka pan rodziny w Polsce.
Andrew	Tak. Wiem, że moi przodkowie pochodzą z Polski.
Ewa	Pana przodkowie mieszkali w Polsce, ale byli Szkotami. Dom rodzinny – stary dwór – jest w Nowych Szkotach.

3 Read the conversations and answer the questions.

a Is Ewa **archeolożką, genealożką** or **antropolożką**?
b Where is Ewa inviting Maria and Andrew?
c What does Andrew know about his family?
d What nationality were Andrew's ancestors?

4 Now read the conversations again and say them out loud as you go along.

Language discovery

DNI TYGODNIA *DAYS OF THE WEEK*

1 Look at the table and study the days of the week.

Dzień tygodnia	English	On Monday, etc.
poniedziałek	*Monday*	**w poniedziałek**
wtorek	*Tuesday*	**we wtorek**
środa	*Wednesday*	**w środę**
czwartek	*Thursday*	**w czwartek**
piątek	*Friday*	**w** ________
sobota	*Saturday*	**w** ________
niedziela	*Sunday*	**w** ________

2 Look at the table again and complete it.

3 Now complete the sentences.

a Spotkamy się (*on Monday*).
b Moje urodziny są (*on Saturday*).
c Mam lekcję angielskiego (*on Wednesday*).
d (*On Tuesday*) będzie padać. (*will be raining*)
e Muszę iść do pracy (*on Friday*).
f Chciałbym iść do galerii handlowej (*on Sunday*).

4 Choose the correct form to complete these sentences.

a Dzisiaj jest (czwartek/czwartku).
b Jutro jest (niedzielę/niedziela).
c Idę na basen (w środa/w środę).
d Test jest (piątek/w piątek).

Go further

MIESIĄCE *MONTHS*

1 Look at the table and study the names of the months. Note the change of spelling in the 'in' form.

Miesiąc (month)	English	In January . . .
styczeń	*January*	**w styczniu**
luty	*February*	**w lutym**
marzec	*March*	**w marcu**
kwiecień	*April*	**w kwietniu**
maj	*May*	**w maju**
czerwiec	*June*	**w czerwcu**
lipiec	*July*	**w lipcu**
sierpień	*August*	**w sierpniu**
wrzesień	*September*	**we wrześniu**
październik	*October*	**w październiku**
listopad	*November*	**w listopadzie**
grudzień	*December*	**w grudniu**

2 Answer the questions in Polish.

a When is your birthday?

in February

in May

in June

b When is Christmas?

in December

c When is Easter?

in March/in April

d When is Polish Independence Day?

in November

MAJ

24

poniedziałek

Joanny Zuzanny

Test yourself

1 Translate the phone conversation into Polish.

You	Hello.
John	John speaking.
You	How are things?
John	Fine, thanks. I've got an interesting (piece of) news.
You	When can we meet? Where can we meet?

2 Say the sentences in Polish.

a What happened?
b Where are we going?
c Let's go!
d Who is it?

3 09.07 **Respond in Polish to the questions and statements. Listen to the recording to check your answers and practice pronunciation.**

	QUESTIONS/STATEMENTS	YOUR RESPONSE
a	**Dokąd idziemy?**	*To Sienna Street.*
b	**O której się spotkamy?**	*At four.*
c	**Do widzenia.**	*See you later.*
d	**Gdzie jest ulica Sienna?**	*Just next to the Market Square.*
e	**Czy ma pan rodzinę w Polsce?**	*I think so.*

SELF CHECK

	I CAN...
●	... ask questions.
●	... indicate time.
●	... arrange a meeting.
●	... describe a location.
●	... indicate frequency.

10

In this unit you will learn how to:

» give and understand street directions.
» describe distances.
» use compass directions such as east and west.

Jak dojechać do ...?

My progress tracker

DAY / DATE	Listen	Speak	Read	Write	Interact
	○	○	○	○	○
	○	○	○	○	○
	○	○	○	○	○
	○	○	○	○	○
	○	○	○	○	○

Finding your way around

Most addresses in Poland have an **ulica** (*a street*) abbreviated to **ul.**, **plac** (*a square*) abbreviated to **pl.** or **aleja/aleje** (*an avenue/avenues*) abbreviated to **al.**, followed by a house number. If an address is in a block of flats, the house number is followed by a slash and a flat number (e.g. 12/4). The slash is sometimes replaced by a letter **m** (short for **mieszkanie**, *a flat*). Some interesting street names in Warsaw are: **Kamienne Schodki** (*Stone Steps*), **Krakowskie Przedmieście** (*Kraków Suburb*), **Nowy Świat** (*New World*), **Krzywe Koło** (*Crooked Circle*). One of the nicest addresses in Warsaw is **ulica Kubusia Puchatka** (*Winnie the Pooh Street*). Roads in the countryside are more often named after a final destination the road leads to, for example **Trakt Krakowski** (*Kraków Highway*), **Droga Staromłyńska** (*Old Mill Road*). But in addition, the countryside is dotted with **figurki** (*small statues*), **kapliczki** (*tiny chapels*) and **krzyże** (*crosses*), used as landmarks and distance markers and all with interesting stories behind them.

Can you translate these addresses?

a Plac Wilsona **b** ulica Krakowska **c** aleja Kwiatowa

Vocabulary builder

10.01 Listen as you look at the words and complete the translations. Then listen again and try to imitate the speakers.

DIRECTIONS

daleko	________
niedaleko	________
blisko	________
prosto	________
w/na prawo	________
w/na lewo	________

COMPASS DIRECTIONS

północ	*north*	na północy Polski	________
południe	*south*	na południu Polski	________
wschód	*east*	na wschodzie Polski	________
zachód	*west*	na zachodzie Polski	________

NEW EXPRESSIONS

jak daleko (jak, daleko)	*how far away*
kiedyś	*ever, at any time, one day*
wiele lat (wiele, rok)	*many years ago*
wypadek	*accident*
droga	*way, path, road*
zamknięta (zamknięty)	*closed*
zawrócić (zawracać > zawrócić)	*turn round, turn back*
pojechać drogą na	*take the road to*
dojechać do + gen. (dojeżdżać > dojechać)	*get to, come up to, reach*
do starego dworu	*to the old manor house*
prosto (prosty)	*straight (on)*
aż do kościoła (kościół)	*right as far as the church*
skręcić w prawo (skręcać > skręcić)	*turn right*
do małego skrzyżowania (mały, skrzyżowanie)	*up to a small crossroads*
przy figurce (przy, figurka)	*by a small statue*
prowadzi do (prowadzić > poprowadzić)	*leads, takes you to*
nie ma za co	*don't mention it, you're welcome*

Do you agree? Answer Yes or No.

a **Na zachód od Krakowa** means *west of Kraków.*

b If someone tells you to **zawrócić**, you should go straight.

Conversations

10.02 *After lunch, Andrew and Maria set off on the short journey to the manor house. It's a warm and sunny afternoon. They leave Kraków behind and drive through the countryside.*

1 How far is it to Nowe Szkoty?

Andrew	Jak daleko są Nowe Szkoty?
Maria	Niedaleko, dwadzieścia kilometrów na zachód od Krakowa.
Andrew	Czy była pani tam kiedyś?
Maria	Tak, wiele lat temu.

10.03 *Suddenly they come to a halt.*

2 Why is the road closed?

Maria	Przepraszam, co się stało?
Policjant	Wypadek. Droga jest zamknięta. Dokąd państwo jadą?
Maria	Do Nowych Szkotów.
Policjant	To muszą państwo zawrócić i pojechać drogą na Tarnów.
Maria	Dobrze. Dziękuję.

3 Read the conversations and answer the questions in Polish.

a Why do Maria and Andrew stop on the road?

b Who does Maria ask what had happened?

c Is Nowe Szkoty east or west of Kraków?

d Has Maria ever been to Nowe Szkoty?

e How can Maria and Andrew get to Nowe Szkoty?

4 Mark the correct answer. Find it in the conversations.

a revised directions to get to Nowe Szkoty:

☐ do Nowych Szkotów ☐ pojechać drogą na Tarnów

b how Maria asks what happened:

☐ Przepraszam, co się stało? ☐ Dokąd państwo jadą?

c how to say *not far*:

☐ niedaleko dwadzieścia ☐ niedaleko

Language discovery

1 ONGOING VS COMPLETED ACTIONS

1 Complete the sentences with the correct form of a word in the box.

napisać zwiedzić kupić obejrzeć gotować zapłacić oglądać usiąść

a Proszę ________ .
b Chciałbym ________ Poznań.
c Można ________ kartą.
d Lubię ________ obiad.
e Trzeba ________ gazetę w kiosku.
f Warto ________ katedrę Świętego Jana (*St John's Cathedral*).
g Lubię ________ filmy.
h Muszę ________ mail.

2 What do you think the following notices say?

a NIE WOLNO PALIĆ.
b TU MOŻNA FOTOGRAFOWAĆ.
c TU WOLNO PARKOWAĆ.

3 Which words go together?

1 gotować	a hotel
2 obejrzeć	b obiad
3 mieszkać	c prezent
4 kupić	d galerie
5 zwiedzać	e film

2 WHY DO POLISH VERBS GO AROUND IN PAIRS?

The short answer is to reflect the difference between actions that have been completed, summed up, rounded off, taken as a whole and actions which are going on at a particular moment or are repeated within a particular period.

Imperfective and perfective

- Verbs that describe ongoing actions are called **imperfective**.
- Verbs that describe completed or packaged actions are called **perfective**.

English usually changes a verb's endings to show these distinctions, but Polish uses different verbs. This is why Polish verbs in vocabulary lists and dictionaries mostly go around in pairs.

Most verbs in this course have been in their perfective form. On the other hand, **lubię** (*I like*) is followed by imperfective verbs, e.g. **lubię gotować** (*I like to cook*).

Look at some examples:

Imperfective	Perfective	English
lubię	**proszę** **muszę** **chciał(a)bym** **trzeba** **warto** **można**	*can I have* *I must/have to* *I'd like to* *you need to* *it's worth* *you can*
gotować	**ugotować**	*to cook*
kupować	**kupić**	*to buy*
czytać	**przeczytać**	*to read*
zwiedzać	**zwiedzić**	*to sightsee*
jeść	**zjeść**	*to eat*
oglądać	**obejrzeć**	*to see/to watch*
pisać	**napisać**	*to write*
płacić	**zapłacić**	*to pay*
rozumieć	**zrozumieć**	*to understand*

Note: There is one more important thing about perfective verbs: they don't have a present tense – you need to use an imperfective verb for that.

It may be helpful to imagine that an imperfective verb films an action going on, whereas a perfective takes a single photo of it.

Practice

1 Choose the correct form to complete the sentences.

a Warto (kupować/kupić) przewodnik.
b Tutaj wolno (siadać/usiąść).
c Mogę (dzwonić/zadzwonić) do domu.
d Lubię (zwiedzać/zwiedzić) Paryż.
e Chciałbym (płacić/zapłacić) gotówką.
f Muszę (widzieć/zobaczyć) ten film.
g Lubię (jeść/zjeść) czekoladę.

2 Put P for perfective or I for imperfective.

a ugotować
b zwiedzić
c zjeść
d zapłacić
e rozumieć
f oglądać

Pronunciation

WORDS WITH DOUBLE CONSONANTS

10.04 When pronouncing words with double consonants, remember: a double letter = double pronunciation. Repeat or prolong the consonant.

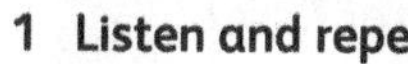

1 Listen and repeat.

hobby	[hob-bi]	*hobby*
Joanna	[joan-na]	*Joanna*
Anna	[an-na]	*Anna*
lekki	[lek-ki]	*light* (opposite of heavy)
Jagiełło	[jagieł-ło]	*Jagiełło* (name of Polish dynastic king)
wanna	[wan-na]	*bathtub*
getto	[get-to]	*ghetto*
miękki	[mienk-ki]	*soft*
willa	[wil-la]	*villa*
ssak	[s-sak]	*mammal*
dziennik	[dzien-nik]	*daily news/journal*

2 Cover the list in Exercise 1 and listen again. Say the sound and name the doubled consonant that you hear.

Conversation

10.05 *Maria and Andrew follow the road towards Tarnów and finally reach Nowe Szkoty.*

1 How does the woman help Maria and Andrew?

Maria	Przepraszam panią, jak dojechać do starego dworu?
Kobieta	Trzeba jechać prosto aż do kościoła. Koło kościoła proszę skręcić w prawo i jechać do małego skrzyżowania przy figurce. Tam proszę skręcić w lewo. Ta droga prowadzi do starego dworu.
Maria	Prosto, do kościoła, w prawo, przy figurce w lewo.
Kobieta	Tak.
Maria	Dobrze. Dziękuję pani bardzo.
Kobieta	Nie ma za co.

2 Now read the conversation and answer the questions in Polish.

- **a** How would you ask how to get to the old manor house?
- **b** How far does Maria need to go straight ahead: to a statue or to a church?
- **c** Where does Maria need to turn left?

3 Nie ma za co means *Thank you very much*. True or false?

4 Imagine your GPS giving you directions as you drive. Write the Polish equivalents.

- **a** Turn left.
- **b** Go straight ahead.
- **c** Turn right.

Language discovery

COMPASS DIRECTIONS

1 Look at the words for compass directions.

północ *north*
na północy Polski
in the north of Poland

zachód *west*
na zachodzie Polski
in the west of Poland

wschód *east*
na wschodzie Polski
in the east of Poland

południe *south*
na południu Polski
in the south of Poland

2 Now describe places in relation to other places.

Example: Windsor is 21 miles west of London. Windsor jest 21 mil na zachód od Londynu.

- **a** Felixstowe is 15 miles east of Ipswich.
- **b** Żelazowa Wola is 60 km west of Warsaw.
- **c** Zakopane is 100 km south of Kraków.
- **d** Scotland is north of England.
- **e** Russia is east of Poland.

Go further

WHERE ARE YOU VS. WHERE ARE YOU RETURNING TO

1 Look at the *where* questions and answers.

Gdzie jesteś? *Where are you?* **W hotelu.** *In the hotel.*

Dokąd wracasz? *Where are you returning to?* **Do hotelu.** *To the hotel.*

2 Study the table and complete the missing forms.

Noun	w/na ... (*in the . . .*)	do ... (*to the . . .*)
hotel	w hotelu	do hotelu
park	w parku	do parku
bank	w banku	________
rynek	na rynku	________
plac	na placu	________
ulica	na ulicy	________
restauracja	w restauracji	________
galeria	w galerii	________
muzeum	________	________

3 Note the spelling will change with certain place names.

Place	w . . .	do . . .
Kraków	w Krakowie	do Krakowa
Londyn (*London*)	w Londynie	do Londynu
Rzym (*Rome*)	w Rzymie	do Rzymu
Paryż (*Paris*)	w Paryżu	do Paryża
Ameryka	w Ameryce	do Ameryki

4 Complete the email from Paris.

Nowa wiadomość

Jestem w ________. Mieszkam w ________ Ritz. Teraz idziemy do ________ d'Orsay. Potem chciałbym zobaczyć wieżę Eiffla. Po południu idziemy do ________ na kolację.

Test yourself

1 Translate the conversations into Polish.

a

You	Excuse me, what happened?
Policjant	An accident. You need to turn round.

b

John	Turn right by the church.
You	No, the road is closed.

2 Complete the sentences.

a Droga jest ________ .

b Przepraszam, co się ________ ?

c Trzeba jechać ________ aż do kościoła.

3 10.06 **Respond in Polish. Listen to the recording to check your answers and practice pronunciation.**

	QUESTIONS	YOUR RESPONSE
a	**Jak daleko jest morze?**	*Not far.*
b	**Czy był pan kiedyś w Stanach?**	*No, but I would like to go there.*
c	**Przepraszam, co się stało?**	*An accident.*

SELF CHECK

	I CAN...
●	... give and understand street directions.
●	... describe distances.
●	... use compass directions such as east and west.

R3 Review 3

1 Complete the conversation with words from the box.

obraz chętnie głodny piwo galerie obrazy obiad kuchnię

Andrew Jestem trochę ________ .
Maria Chodźmy na ________ . Czy lubi pan ________ polską?
Andrew Tak, lubię bigos, sernik i polskie ________ .
Maria Czy lubi pan ________ Leonarda da Vinci?
Andrew Tak, bardzo. Dlaczego pani pyta?
Maria W Krakowie jest słynny ________ Leonarda, *Dama z łasiczką*. Czy chciałby pan go zobaczyć?
Andrew Bardzo ________ . Lubię zwiedzać ________ i muzea.

2 Make sentences. Match the beginnings with the endings.

a Szkoda, że nie wolno
b Można kupić widokówki
c Proszę iść prosto
d Można zapłacić

1 albo gotówką albo kartą.
2 robić zdjęć w galerii.
3 w sklepie muzealnym.
4 korytarzem do wyjścia.

3 What kind of question is it? *What, Who, Where* or *When*?

a Co to jest? To jest przystanek autobusowy.
b Kto to jest? To jest Handa.
c Gdzie to jest? To jest w kinie.
d Kiedy to jest? To jest w sobotę.

4 Part of an email message got deleted. Try to reconstruct it.

Nowa wiadomość

Cześć,

Muszę się z tobą ______. Mam bardzo intersesującą ______ dla ciebie. Może spotkamy się o t______ciej przy muzeum.

Do ______

Kuba

5 Translate the extract from the Polish guidebook into English.

Kolekcja Czartoryskich w Krakowie to bardzo interesujące muzeum. Można tam zobaczyć słynne obrazy – *Dama z łasiczką* Leonarda da Vinci i *Pejzaż z Dobrym Samarytaninem* Rembrandta. Niestety, cenny obraz Raphaela – *Portret Młodzieńca* – zaginął. Jest tajemnicą co się z nim stało.

6 Replace the words in brackets with the correct Polish words from the box.

polską indyjska chińska włoską
lubię francuska meksykańskiej hiszpańska
tajwańska kuchnię kuchni tajskiej grecką

a (*I like*) kuchnię francuską.
b Do you like (*Greek cuisine*)?
c Lubię muzykę (*Italian*).
d Do you want to go to a (*Mexican*) restaurant?
e He likes the peanut sauce in (*Thai*) food.

7 Translate the following into Polish.

a I'd like to have a look at the old films. (**stare filmy**)

b What kind of manor house is it?

c Here you are, here's a map.

d Can we go to the cinema this afternoon?

8 Where have the following emails been sent from?

Nowa wiadomość

Pozdrowienia z ____________ .

Dzisiaj zwiedzamy Galerię Narodową i Muzeum Brytyjskie.

Nowa wiadomość

Pozdrowienia z ________ .

Jestem tu na weekend. Chciałabym zwiedzić Luwr, ale mam mało czasu.

Nowa wiadomość

Pozdrowienia z ________ .

To piękne miasto kanałów, diamentów i obrazów Rembrandta!

9 Choose the correct word to complete the sentence.

a Sherlock Holmes jest (aktorem/pisarzem/detektywem).

b Łódź to duże (miasto/wioska/stolica).

c Atlanta jest na (wschodzie/zachodzie/północy/południu) Stanów Zjednoczonych.

d Wawel jest w (Krakowie/Warszawie/Poznaniu).
e Kamienne Schodki to (plac/aleja/ulica) w Warszawie.

10 Do you agree? Answer Yes or No.

a **Jestem Kacper** means *My surname is Kacper.*
b **Wejście** means *exit.*
c **Lubię czekoladę** means *I like drinking tea.*
d **Poproszę czekoladę** means *Can I have some chocolate please?*

11 Choose the correct answer.

a If you want to ask for coffee, you would say:
1 Poproszę kawę. 2 Poproszę herbatę. 3 Piwo proszę.
b You would say **Przepraszam** if you want to:
1 apologize 2 ask for something 3 both 1 and 2
c If you want to ask what time it is, you would say:
1 O której godzinie? 2 Która godzina? 3 Na którą godzinę?
d If you want to say you'll meet on Friday, you'd use:
1 w poniedziałek 2 w niedzielę 3 w piątek

12 Look at the menu. Fill in the blanks with correct Polish headings.

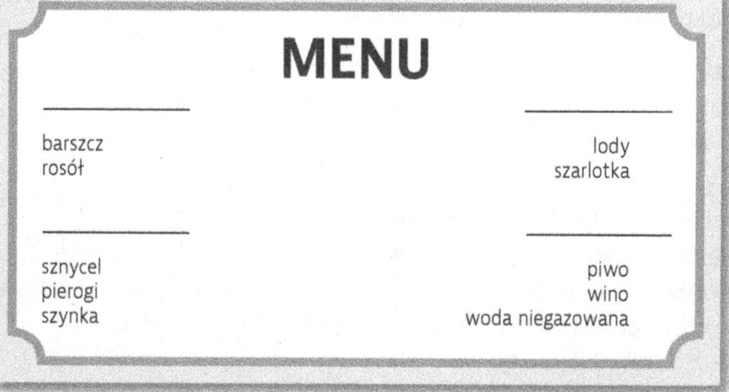

13 A friend is visiting you. Give the directions to your house in Polish.

You need to go straight on to the bank. Then turn left into Station St – go straight ahead. Turn right by the church. Go as far as the crossroads. Turn left – my house is on the right. Number 24.

Answer key

UNIT 1

Greeting people in Polish
dobry (dobra), wieczór, noc

Vocabulary builder
Greetings and salutations: good morning or afternoon, good evening, good night, goodbye, man, pleased
New expressions: a No, **b** No, **c** Yes

Conversation
1 Jestem
2 a daytime, **b** good morning/afternoon, **c** Pleased to meet you – to respond to Maria's greeting, **d** Please come in, **e** Please sit down, **f** Nie jestem głodny. **g** Czy jest pan zmęczony? or informally – Czy jesteś zmęczony? **h** Yes, a bit.
3 a nie, **b** tak, **c** zmęczony, **d** głodny

Language discovery
a jestem, **b** jest pan, **c** pani

Practice
a Polką, **b** Irlandczykiem, **c** pracowita, **d** zajęty
2 a F, **b** F, **c** T, **d** F

Conversation
1 Describing nationality and professions
2 a Jestem Polką. **b** I've got Scottish (family) roots, **c** Czy jest pan Szkotem czy Anglikiem? or informally Czy jesteś Szkotem czy Anglikiem? **d** Jestem prywatnym detektywem. **e** Czym się pani zajmuje?, **f** half, **g** No
3 a 4, **b** 3, **c** 1, **d** 2

Language discovery

Table: On jest zmęczony/ona jest zmęczona/ono jest zmęczone/pan jest zmęczony/pani jest zmęczona

Go further

2 a Adam – Anglik/student, **b** Josh – Kanadyjczyk/artysta, **c** Ingrid – Argentynka/dziennikarka

Test yourself

1 a Dzień dobry. **b** Bardzo mi miło. **c** Jestem Maria Grajewska. **d** Proszę wejść. **e** Proszę usiąść. **f** Czy jest pan zmęczony?

2 a Polką, **b** Proszę wejść

3 a Nie jestem głodny. **b** On nie jest zmęczony.

4 a Bardzo mi miło. **b** Dziękuję. **c** Tak, trochę. **d** Jestem na emeryturze./ Jestem emerytem (masc.)/emerytką (fem.).

UNIT 2

Pets in Poland

zły pies – bad dog; sheepdog – owczarek

Vocabulary builder

Describing animals: to jest – this is/it is; pies – dog; dobry – good; zły – bad/angry (dog)

New expressions: a doctor – medycynę, **b** not good – zły, **c** mother – rodzina, **d** a way to learn – studiuje, **e** not bad – dobry

Conversations

1 No, Azor is a good dog.

2 Molly is Andrew's daughter. Thomas is Andrew's father.

3 a To jest mój pies. **b** Czy to jest zły pies? **c** Molly studiuje medycynę. **d** Thomas, **e** Who is this?

4 a Yes, **b** Yes, **c** No, **d** No

Language discovery
a córka, **b** emerytką, **c** Kto

Practice
1 a F, **b** M, **c** M, **d** F
2 a Y, **b** N, **c** N, **d** Y
3 a Ona jest studentką, **b** On jest detektywem. **c** One są Angielkami

Pronunciation
3 mapa / pot / Europa / pogotowie / karta / poczta

Conversation
1 Jakub is Maria's father.
2 a mama, **b** ojciec, **c** dziadek
3 a Tomasz, **b** To jest moja mama, Teresa. **c** Kto to jest?
4 b To jest moja żona.

Practice
1 a moja mama, **b** moja córka, **c** mój ojciec, **d** mój dziadek, **e** mój brat
2 a mój/twój pies, **b** mój/twój ojciec, **c** moja/twoja mama, **d** moja/twoja córka
3 a To jest jego pies. **b** To jest jej córka. **c** To jest twój ojciec. **d** To jest mój brat.

Go further
Examples:
mój + brat = mój brat (masculine), moja + żona = moja żona (feminine), moje + dziecko = moje dziecko (neuter)
a, c, d

Test yourself
1a To jest mój pies, Toffee. **b** To jest bardzo dobry pies. **c** Czy to jest twoja rodzina? **d** Tak, to jest moja żona i córka. **e** Jest bardzo ładna. **f** Molly jest studentką. **g** Studiuje medycynę. **h** Kto to jest? **i** To jest mój dziadek, Jakub. **j** Czy to jest twoja mama? **k** Co to jest? **l** To jest moja rodzina.
2 a ładna, **b** córka, **c** medycynę, **d** pies
3 Examples: To jest moja mama, żona, siostra, córka. To jest mój tata/ tato (ojciec), mąż, brat, syn.
4 a To jest mój ojciec. **b** (Ona) Studiuje medycynę. **c** Bardzo mi miło. **d** Nie, to (jest) dobry pies.

UNIT 3

Family life in Poland

dziadek – dziadkowie (grandfather/grandparents)

Vocabulary builder

Borrowed words: photographs, contacts, address, architect

New expressions: a w, **b** imię, **c** nazwisko

Conversation

1 Surname and an address

2 a Yes, he does. (Tak, Andrew ma czas na herbatę.) **b** Yes, he does. (Tak, Andrew ma dokumenty rodzinne.) **c** Mam kontakty w Archiwum. **d** That's no problem at all.

3 No way!

Language discovery

a ma, **b** mam, **c** ma, **d** ma

Practice: a ma, **b** masz, **c** mam (or ma), **d** ma, **e** ma

Conversation

1 He's an architect.

2 a husband/son (mąż/syn) **b** He's got a good job and money. (On ma dobra pracę i pieniądze.) **c** He hasn't got children. (On nie ma dzieci.) **d** Her husband's name is Piotr. (Jej mąż ma na imię Piotr.) **e** He's retired. (On jest na emeryturze.)

4 rodzinę/mam/syna/syn/pracę/ale/dzieci

Practice

1 a architektem, **b** pieniądze, **c** czasu, **d** dobrą, pracę, **e** męża i syna

2 Should be: **a** Mam dokument or Nie mam dokumentu, **b** Maria ma rodzinę or Maria nie ma rodziny, **c** Nie mam czasu or Mam czas, **d** Mam ochotę na herbatę or Nie mam ochoty na herbatę, **e** Ile ma pani lat?

3 a rodzinę, **b** rodziny, **c** Jaki, **d** Jaka

Go further

1 a dokument, **b** dokumentu, **c** dziecko, **d** dziecka, **e** czas, **f** czas, **g** psa, **h** fotografia, **i** fotografii

2 c Nie mam dokumentu.

Test yourself

1 a Mam rodzinę w Polsce. **b** Mam problem. **c** Mam ochotę na herbatę. **d** Czy masz/ma pan/ma pani jakieś kontakty w Archiwum? **e** Nie mam czasu. **f** Mam dużo czasu. **g** Moja córka ma dobrą pracę. **h** Mam psa, Rexa. **i** Mam dwadzieścia lat.

2 a Chyba tak. **b** Jaki problem? **c** Tak, mam dużo czasu. **d** Tak, mam (ochotę).
3 a Nie mam czasu. **b** Mój syn nie jest architektem. **c** Nie mają psa.
d To nie jest mój ojciec.
4 a Kim pani jest/Czym się pani zajmuje? **b** Kto to jest? **c** Czy masz/ma pan/ma pani dokumenty? **d** Czy Azor to (jest) zły pies?

UNIT 4

About time in Poland

czas to pieniądz – time is money; kwadrans akademicki = 15 minutes

Vocabulary builder

Time and necessity: necessarily, have to, must, potem, do, załatwić
New expressions: a, c

Conversation

1 It's four o'clock.
2 a Andrew musi załatwić kilka spraw. (... has to get a few things), **b** Yes. (Tak.), **c** Musi pan też zwiedzić Kraków. (... must visit Krakow), **d** O tak, koniecznie. (Yes), **e** Bardzo chętnie. **f** unfortunately
3 a 3, **b** 4, **c** 2, **d** 1, **e** 5

Language discovery

a Która godzina? **b** Co musi pan/pani/musisz zrobić? **c** Czy musisz/musi pan/pani zobaczyć Kraków?

Practice

1 a musi, **b** muszą, **c** musisz, **d** musimy
2 pierwsza, piąta, szósta, jedenasta

Pronunciation

2 a niebo, **b** dzień, **c** łokieć, **d** list, **e** ciało, **f** biały
3 n, dz, k, l, c, b

Listen and understand

Telling the time: 2 a trzecia, **b** dziewiąta, **c** druga
3
a
Ines: Przepraszam, która godzina?
Dawid: Siódma wieczorem.

b
Vadim: Przepraszam, która godzina?
Natalia: Czwarta po południu.
c
Jingyi: Przepraszam, która godzina?
Staś: Dziesiąta wieczorem.
At what time: (4:00) – o czwartej; (5.00) – o piątej; (6.00) – o szóstej; (7.00) – o siódmej; (8.00) – o ósmej; (9.00) – o dziewiątej; (10.00) – o dziesiątej; (11.00) – o jedenstej; (12.00) – o dwunastej
4 See answers above.

Go further

1 a Muszę rozpakować się w hotelu *or* W hotelu muszę się rozpakować, **b** On musi się golić codziennie *or* On musi się codziennie golić, **c** Ona się musi myć rano *or* Ona rano musi się myć
2 a Muszę się rozpakować or Rozpakować się muszę, **b** Maria i Andrew muszą zwiedzić Kraków, **c** Przepraszam, która godzina?

Test yourself

1a Muszę już iść. **b** Dlaczego musisz/musi pan/musi pani iść? **c** Ona musi wrócić do jej hotelu. **d** Muszę zadzwonić do domu. **e** Musisz zwiedzić/zobaczyć Londyn. **f** Musimy spotkać się znowu. **g** Bardzo chętnie. **h** O tak, koniecznie.
2 a Bardzo chętnie. **b** O tak, koniecznie. **c** Szkoda. **d** Tak, mam. **e** Nazywam się . . .
3 a czwartej, **b** się, **c** pieniądze, **d** godzina, **e** spraw

UNIT 5

Visiting Poland

informacja turystyczna – tourist information;
kopalnie – mines

Vocabulary builder

Borrowed words: reception, restaurant, information, transformation
New expressions: **a** No, **b** No, **c** No

Conversations

1 Tomorrow.
2 Andrew would like to book a table in a hotel restaurant.
3 a Not at all/you're welcome, **b** Rozumiem, **c** 125, **d** na siódmą trzydzieści (7:30), **e** słucham, **f** Dzień dobry, recepcja, słucham, **g** Na którą godzinę?

Language discovery

3 5:00 na piątą; 6:00 – na szóstą; 7:00 – na siódmą; 8:00 – na ósmą; 9:00 – na dziewiątą; 10:00 – na dziesiątą; 11:00 – na jedenastą; 12:00 – na dwunastą

Practice

1 a siódmej, **b** czwartej, **c** dziewiątej, **d** trzeciej, **e** szóstą, **f** pierwszą, **g** dwunasta
2 a w Krakowie, **b** Wawelu, **c** informacji, **d** psa, **e** stolik, **f** przewodnik

Listen and understand

2 a find documents, **b** meet Ewa
3 a się, **b** Chciałabym, informacji, dokumenty
4 a 4, **b** 3, **c** 1, **d** 2

Consonants and consonants

3 a moment, **b** może, **c** rachunek, **d** chętnie, **e** czas, **f** szkoła, **g** archiwum, **h** architekt, **i** schody, **j** kuchnia, **k** deszcz, **l** szczur

Go further

2 a sześćset dwa, siedemset czterdzieści trzy, pięćset jedenaście,
b sześćset trzy, sto dwadzieścia jeden, dziewięćset,
c pięćset dwa, trzysta osiemdziesiąt, pięćset piętnaście,
d pięćset trzy, siedemset pięćdziesiąt, sto dziewiętnaście

Test yourself

1 a Dziękuję za spotkanie. **b** Chciałbym znaleźć moją rodzinę. **c** Chciał(a) bym zamówić stolik. **d** Poproszę nazwisko. **e** Co słychać? **f** Na którą godzinę? **g** Na siódmą trzydzieści. **h** Chciał(a)bym spotkać się z tobą/z panem/z panią.

2 a Nie chciałbym zamówić stolika. **b** Nie chciałabym kupić przewodnika. **c** Nie muszę zobaczyć Wawelu. **d** Nie mam konia. **e** Nie chciałbym wymienić pieniędzy. **f** Nie muszę zrobić zakupów. **g** Nie jestem głodny.

3 a Jakiej pomocy? **b** Poproszę adres. **c** Nie, jestem Szkotem. **d** O której godzinie?

UNIT 6

Foods and cuisine

mięso: wołowina/wieprzowina/szynka/kotlet schabowy (aka sznycel)

Vocabulary builder

Paying the check: Can I help you?/I'd like the check/OK/How much?

New expressions: 1 a rachunek, **b** zapłacić, **c** kelner; **2 a** No, **b** No, **c** No

Conversations

1 Maria orders coffee and cheesecake and Andrew orders tea and ice cream.

2 Maria asks for the check.

3 a True, **b** False, **c** False, **d** False

Language discovery

1, 2 a hamburger (m), **b** cheese (m), **c** milk (n);
d vodka (f), **e** gateau (m), **f** mineral water (f), **g** tomato soup (f), **h** yoghurt (m), **i** chocolate (f)

Practice

1 a bilet, **b** rachunek, **c** zupę

2 a No, **b** Yes, **c** No

3 a False, **b** False, **c** False

4 a dania mięsne, **b** zupy, **c** desery, **d** zupy, **e** desery, **f** dania wegetariańskie, **g** alkohole

5 a rachunek, **b** sernik, **c** barszcz *or* rosół, **d** wino

Pronunciation

1 a deszcz, **b** schody, **c** gwóźdź, **d** drzewo, **e** skrzypce, **f** dość, **g** kość, **h** chrzan, **i** przepraszam

2 a deszcz, **b** kość *or* dość, **c** krzyczeć *or* większy

Listen and understand

2 c

3 b (2.50)

4 **a** widokówkę/Proszę. **b** płacę/Dwa

At the kiosk:

5 a Poproszę czasopismo, **b** . . . notatnik, **c** . . . gazetę

Reading, writing and speaking

2 a post office, **b** postal assistant, **c** stamp

3 Answers will vary.

Go further

2 a Czy mogę prosić o dokumenty? **b** Sok proszę, **c** Czy mogę prosić o sok? **d** Poproszę herbatę, **e** Herbatę proszę, **f** Czy mogę prosić o herbatę? **g** Poproszę reklamówkę, **h** Reklamówkę proszę, **i** Czy mogę prosić o reklamówkę?, **j** Poproszę znaczek, **k** Znaczek proszę, **l** Czy mogę prosić o znaczek?, **m** Poproszę rachunek, **n** Rachunek proszę, **o** Czy mogę prosić o rachunek?

Test yourself

1 a Poproszę kawę. **b** Poproszę sernik. **c** Chciał(a)bym zapłacić rachunek. **d** Wykluczone. Jesteś moim gościem. **e** Poproszę znaczek priorytetowy do Wielkiej Brytanii. **f** Jestem wegetarianinem. **g** Mam alergię na orzechy.

2 a Poproszę herbatę. **b** Poproszę kawę. **c** Poproszę znaczek. **d** Poproszę przewodnik. **e** Chciał(a)bym herbatę. **f** Chciał(a)bym kawę. **g** Chciał(a) bym kupić znaczek. **h** Chciał(a)bym kupić przewodnik.

3 a emerytem – wrong gender; should be emerytką. **b** Polką – wrong gender; should be Polakiem. **c** kawa – wrong case; should be (acc.) kawę. **d** znaczek – wrong noun; should be stolik. **e** jestem – wrong verb; should be Mam. **f** herbata – wrong case; should be herbatę. **g** kupić – wrong verb; should be zwiedzić or zobaczyć.

4 a Proszę. **b** Poproszę kawę. **c** Wykluczone. Jesteś moim gościem. **d** Dwa złote pięćdziesiąt groszy.

UNIT 7

What, where and when to eat

c kanapka

Vocabulary builder

More borrowed words: gallery; museum
About art: famous; go
Words you may remember: hungry; beer; cheesecake
New expressions:
1 a famous, **b** No (**rynek** means 'market'), **c** No. **Sukiennice** is a place to visit or buy souvenirs, **d** No, (it means 'I'm a bit hungry')

Conversations

1 Andrew likes bigos, cheesecake and Polish beer/lager
2 Places to see in Kraków
3 a Jestem (trochę) głodny. **b** Hunters' stew **c** cheesecake and Polish beer **d** Rynek, Sukiennice, Wawel i Muzeum Narodowe
4
a (Andrew:) bigos, **b** (You:) Chciał(a)bym zobaczyć
5 a obiad – kuchnia, **b** rynek – galeria

Language discovery

2 Lubię kuchnię francuską/meksykańską/hiszpańską/tajwańską/tajską/grecką

Practice

1 a dworzec kolejowy, **b** straż pożarna, **c** aparat słuchowy

2 a beauty salon, **b** mechanical device, **c** Język, **d** salon fryzjerski

3 a kuchnia chińska, **b** kuchnia włoska, **c** kuchnia indyjska, **d** kuchnia polska, **e** kuchnia meksykańska

Pronunciation

2 a [f], **b** [sz]

3 a t, **b** k, **c** s, **d** p, **e** ch, **f** k

5 a trzeba, **b** twarz, **c** przyloty, **d** wszystko, **e** chrzan, **f** przepraszam

Conversation

1 Painting by Leonardo can be seen in Kraków.

2 a 'Dama z łasiczką', **b** Tak, Andrew lubi obrazy Leonarda da Vinci, **c** Andrew lubi zwiedzać muzea. **d** Yes

3 a Tak, bardzo, **b** słynny obraz, **c** Czy lubisz/lubi pan/lubi pani?

Language discovery

a Yes, **b** No, **c** No

Go further

2 b–p / d–t / g–k / ż–sz / rz–sz / dż–cz

3 a grzyb [grzyp], **b** dąb [domp], **c** lew [lef], **d** twarz [tfasz]

Test yourself

1 a Czy lubisz/lubi pan/lubi pani polską kuchnię?

b Co chciał(a)byś/chciałby pan/chciałaby pani zobaczyć/zwiedzić w Krakowie?

c Chciał(a)bym zobaczyć Rynek i Sukiennice.

d Lubię kuchnię chińską, ale nie lubię kuchni indyjskiej.

2 a pić, **b** czekoladę, **c** słuchać, **d** oglądać

3 1 e, **2** c, **3** h, **4** j, **5** l, **6** b or m, **7** b or m, **8** i, **9** k, **10** g, **11** f, **12** a, **13** d

4 a Tak, lubię. **b** Lubię kuchnię polską i (kuchnię) włoską.

UNIT 8

Discovering mysteries in Poland

The mystery of the amber treasure.

Vocabulary builder

Shopping at a museum shop: magnet, coffee table book, guide, poster, bookmark, credit card, postcard, book

New expressions: a wolno, **b** trzeba, **c** przykro mi

Conversation

1 Take photos

2 a pity, **b** a guidebook, **c** in the museum store

3 a book

Language discovery

a Można robić zdjęcia, **b** obrazy, **c** kalendarz/kalendarze, **d** Wolno wejść

Practice

1 Answers will vary (All choices could be correct.)

2 a domy, **b** koty, **c** numery, **d** adresy, **e** serniki, **f** hotele, **g** kraje, **h** rachunki

3 a soki, **b** kroki, **c** talerze, **d** worki, **e** samoloty

Pronunciation

3 a False, **b** True, **c** True

Conversations

1 yes, it is on the ground floor

2 with a credit card

3 a No **b** No **c** Yes **d** Yes

4 a nie wiem (The other two are directions.) **b** można (The other two explain where something is.) **c** gdzie (The other two are verbs.) **d** co (The other two are prepositions of place.)

Language discovery

2 a gotówką/kartą zbliżeniową/kartą kredytową, **b** kartą zbliżeniową/karta kredytową/gotówką, **c** reszta, **d** bankomat

3 a gotówka, **b** change, **c** bankomat, **d** karta zbliżeniowa, **e** credit card

4 coins

Go further

2 (Andrew:) wyjść (Maria) korytarzem, do sklepu, prosto, w dół, na parterze (Andrew) w sklepie

3 Answers will vary.

Test yourself

1 a telefony, **b** komputery, **c** samochody

2 a Czy wolno robić zdjęcia w muzeum? **b** Przykro mi, ale nie wolno. **c** Szkoda. **d** Co jeszcze można tam kupić?

3 a Nie, nie wolno. **b** Na parterze. **c** W sklepie muzealnym.

4 a zobaczyć/obejrzeć/zrobić, **b** sklep, **c** kartą kredytową,

UNIT 9

Celebrations

b rocznica ślubu

Vocabulary builder

Asking and answering questions: what's happened, how are you (doing)?, what (sort)?, where (to)?, explain, on the way, not far (from), next to, next

New expressions: **c** co słychać

Conversations

1 Maria has an interesting piece of news for Andrew.

2 Ewa's office is in Sienna Street next to the Market Square.

3 a False, **b** False, **c** False, **d** True

4 a Co się stało?, **b** Gdzie?, **c** O której?

Language discovery

a Co to jest?, **b** Kto to jest?, **c** Co to jest?, **d** Gdzie to jest?

Practice

1 c wieczorem

2 b często / **c** czasami / **d** rzadko / **a** nigdy

3 a Yes, **b** Yes, **c** Yes

Pronunciation

3 second syllable from the end (penultimate) syllable
4 third syllable from the end

Conversations

1 Ewa works at the archive office.
2 Ewa knows that Andrew is searching for his family.
3 a Ewa jest genealożką. (Ewa is a genealogist.) **b** She is inviting them to go to her office. **c** He knows that his family comes from Poland. **d** His ancestors were Scots.

Language discovery

2 w piątek/w sobotę/w niedzielę
3 a w poniedziałek, **b** w sobotę, **c** w środę, **d** We wtorek, **e** w piątek, **f** w niedzielę
4 a czwartek, **b** niedziela, **c** w środę, **d** w piątek

Go further

2 a w lutym/w maju w czerwcu, **b** w grudniu, **c** w marcu/w kwietniu, **d** w listopadzie

Test yourself

1
You: Słucham.
John: Mówi John.
You: Co słychać?
John: Dobrze, dziękuję. Mam interesującą wiadomość.
You: Kiedy możemy się spotkać? Gdzie możemy się spotkać?
2 a Co się stało? **b** Dokąd idziemy? **c** Chodźmy. **d** Kto to jest?
3 a Na ulicę Sienną. **b** O czwartej. **c** Do zobaczenia. **d** Tuż obok Rynku. **e** Chyba tak.

UNIT 10

Finding your way around

a Wilson Square, **b** Kraków Street, **c** Flower Avenue

Vocabulary builder

Directions:

far, not far, near, straight on, (turn) right/on the right, (turn) left/on the left

Compass directions:

in the north of Poland, in the south of Poland, in the east of Poland, in the west of Poland

New expressions: a Yes, **b** No

Conversations

1 It's 20 km to Nowe Szkoty.

2 The road is closed because of an accident.

3 a Droga jest zamknięta. **b** Maria pyta policjanta. **c** Na zachód od Krakowa **d** Tak, wiele lat temu. **e** Maria i Andrew muszą zawrócić i pojechać drogą na Tarnów.

4 a pojechać drogą na Tarnów, **b** Przepraszam, co się stało? **c** niedaleko

Language discovery

1 a usiąść, **b** zwiedzić/obejrzeć, **c** zapłacić, **d** gotować, **e** kupić, **f** zwiedzić/obejrzeć, **g** oglądać, **h** napisać

2 a No smoking, **b** Photographs allowed (permitted), **c** Parking allowed (permitted)

3 1 b, **2** e, **3** a, **4** c, **5** d

Practice

1 a kupić, **b** siadać/usiąść, **c** zadzwonić, **d** zwiedzać, **e** zapłacić, **f** zobaczyć, **g** jeść

2 a P, **b** P, **c** P, **d** P, **e** I, **f** I

Conversation

1 She gives them directions to the old manor house.

2 a Przepraszam, jak dojechać do starego dworu?

b Aż do kościoła.

c Przy figurce.

3 False

4 a Skręcić w lewo. **b** Jechać prosto. **c** Skręcić w prawo.

Language discovery

2

a Felixstowe jest 15 mil na wschód od Ipswich.

b Żelazowa Wola jest 60 km na zachód od Warszawy.

c Zakopane jest 100 km na południe od Krakowa.

d Szkocja jest na północ od Anglii.

e Rosja jest na wschód od Polski.

Go further

2

do banku / do rynku / do placu / do ulicy /
do restauracji / do galerii / w muzeum / do muzeum

4 Paryżu / hotelu / muzeum / restauracji

Test yourself

1 a

You: Przepraszam, co się stało?

Policjant: Wypadek. Trzeba zawrócić.

b

John: Trzeba skręcić w prawo przy kościele.

You: Nie, droga jest zamknięta.

2 a zamknięta, **b** stało, **c** prosto

3 a Niedaleko. **b** Nie, ale chciałbym tam pojechać. **c** Wypadek.

REVIEWS

R1 (Units 1–3)

1 a Hanna Kosińska, **b** Tomasz Dąbrowski, **c** Aleksander Kosiarski, **d** Ewa Kowalska, **e** Krzysztof Jakubowski, **f** Jakub Paderewski, **g** Julia Słomczyńska, **h** Amelia Jaworska

2 a I am Kuba Kowalczyk or My name is Kuba Kowalczyk. **b** Pleased to meet you. **c** I'm not Polish. I'm English. **d** I've got Polish roots. **e** Andrzej is retired. **f** Maria is Polish. **g** What do you do (for a living)?

3 a M, **b** F, **c** M, **d** F, **e** M, **f** F

4 a mój pies, **b** mój kot, **c** moja rodzina, **d** To jest, **e** medycynę, **f** studentką, **g** To, **h** wysoka, **i** wysoką dziewczyną, **j** miły, **k** to

5 a rodzinę, **b** rodziny, **c** Jaki, **d** Jaki, **e** Żadna, **f** jakieś, **g** dokumenty/fotografie, **h** na **i** adresu, **j** adres, **k** na, **l** emerytką, **m** emeryt, **n** samochodu

6 a Tomek is advertising a vacant room. **b** Tomek studies medicine.

7a lampa F, **b** samochód M, **c** radio N, **d** telefon M, **e** herbata F, **f** kobieta F, **g** dziecko N, **h** dom M, **i** autobus M, **j** tramwaj M, **k** tulipan M, **l** mapa F, **m** piwo N

R2 (Units 4–6)

1 a What do you have to do, sir? **b** I must/have to return home. **c** We must/have to meet. **d** We must/have to. **e** I must/have to see Warsaw. **f** No, you don't have to, sir. **g** I want to have some coffee. **h** Absolutely!

2 a musi, **b** muszą, **c** musisz, **d** musimy, **e** pan, **f** spotkać, **g** zwiedzić

3 a On przeprasza. **b** Oni/One przepraszają. **c** (My) przepraszamy. **d** Dlaczego ona nie przeprasza?

4 a na, **b** do, **c** w, **d** za, **e** w, **f** Na, **g** Do, **h** Do, **i** z, **j** w

5 a zwiedzić, **b** zrobić, **c** pomocy, **d** zamówić, **e** przewodnika, **f** czekają

6 e / d / c / b / a

7 a F, **b** T, **c** F, **d** T, **e** F, **f** T, **g** F

8 a O której zaczyna się film? **b** Która godzina? **c** Na którą godzinę? **d** O której chciałbyś przyjśc? **e** O której musisz wyjść?

9 a 2, **b** 4, **c** 1, **d** 3

10 spotkanie / chciałbym / rozumiem / zobaczenia

11 a Jestem detektywem or Jestem architektem.
b Nie, Toffik to dobry pies or Tak, Toffik to zły pies.
c Chciałbym zwiedzić Muzeum Narodowe or Chciałbym zwiedzić Wawel.
d Mam . . . lat(a).

12 Job as a childminder.
13 a Natalia, **b** Yes, she can, **c** Renaissance and Baroque art, **d** nervous patients
14 a Krajewska should be Krajewski, **b** masz should be ma, **c** chciałby should be chciałaby, **d** muszę should be musi
15 a informacji, **b** pomocy, **c** dokumenty, **d** prezent, **e** muzeum, **f** zdjęcie, **g** herbaty

R3 (Units 7–10)

1 głodny / obiad / kuchnię / piwo / obrazy / obraz / chętnie / galerie
2 a 2, **b** 3, **c** 4, **d** 1
3 a what, **b** who, **c** where, **d** when
4 spotkać / wiadomość or informację / trzeciej / zobaczenia
5 The Czartoryski Collection is a very interesting museum. You can see some famous paintings – 'Lady with the Ermine' by Leonardo da Vinci and 'The Landscape with the Good Samaritan' by Rembrandt. Unfortunately, a precious painting by Raphael – 'Portrait of a Young Man' – got lost. It is a mystery what happened to it.
6 a Lubię, **b** kuchnię grecką, **c** włoską, **d** meksykańskiej, **e** kuchni tajskiej
7 a Chciał(a)bym obejrzeć stare filmy. **b** Co to za dwór? **c** Proszę, to jest mapa. **d** Czy możemy pójść do kina dziś po południu?
8 Londynu / Paryża / Amsterdamu
9 a detektywem, **b** miasto, **c** południu, **d** Krakowie, **e** ulica
10 a No, **b** No, **c** No, **d** Yes
11 a 1, **b** 3, **c** 2, **d** 3
12
zupy, desery, dania główne, napoje
13
Prosze iść prosto do banku. Potem proszę skręcić w lewo w ulicę Dworcową – proszę iść prosto. Proszę skręcić w prawo przy kościele. Proszę iść aż do skrzyżowania. Potem skręcić w lewo – mój dom jest po prawej stronie. Numer 24.

Polish–English glossary

a *and (with a change of participant), and/but*
A to? *And (what about) this?*
adresu (adres) *address*
albumy (album) *albums*
Anglicy (Anglik) *English people*
Anglikiem (Anglik) *Englishman*
ani ... ani ... *neither . . . nor . . .*
architektem (architekt) *architect*
archiwistką (archiwistka) *archivist (female)*
archiwum *archive(s)*
Argentynka *Argentinian (woman)*
Argentyńczyk *Argentinian (man)*
artysta (m) / artystka (f) *artist*
aż do kościoła (kościół) *as far as the church*

bardzo *very*
bardzo chętnie *very happily, willingly, would love to*
Bardzo mi miło. (ja, miły) *Pleased to meet you.*
bigos *traditional Polish cabbage stew known as hunters' stew*
Brazylijczyk *Brazilian (man)*
Brazylijka *Brazilian (woman)*
być *to be*
byli (być) *they were*

chętnie (chętny) *willingly, with pleasure*
chodź (chodzić > pochodzić) *come on*
chodźmy (chodzić > pochodzić) *let's go*
chyba *I think, I suppose*
ciekawe (ciekawy) *interesting*
co się stało (stawać się > stać się) *what's happened*
Co słychać? *How are things? What's new?*
córka *daughter*
czas na + acc. *time for*
cześć *hi*
czwarta (czwarty) *four o'clock (the fourth hour)*
czy *word used to introduce a yes/no question; or*
Czym się pan/pani zajmuje? *What do you do for a living / What are you doing?*

dama *lady (poetic)*
detektywem (detektyw) *detective*
dla + gen. *for, for the sake of*
dla ciebie (dla, ty) *for you*
dlaczego *why*
do + gen. *to*
do małego skrzyżowania (mały, skrzyżowanie) *up to a small crossroads*
do mojego biura (do, mój, biuro) *to my office*
do sklepu (sklep) *to the shop*
do starego dworu (do, stary, dwór) *to the old manor house*
do widzenia (widzenie; widzieć > zobaczyć) *goodbye (till we see each other)*
do Wielkiej Brytanii (Wielka Brytania) *to Great Britain*
do zobaczenia (zobaczenie; widzieć > zobaczyć) *see you*
dobrą pracę (dobra, praca) *a good job*
dobry *good*
dobrze (dobry) *OK, correctly, well, right*
dojechać do + gen. (dojeżdżać > dojechać) *get to, come up to, reach*

dokąd *where (to)*
dokumenty (dokument) *documents*
domu (dom) *home, house*
droga *way, path, road*
dużo *a lot*
dwa pięćdziesiąt *two fifty*
dworu (dwór) *of the manor house*
dziadek *grandfather*
dzieci (dziecko) *children*
dzień *day*
dzień dobry (dzień, dobry) *hello, good morning, good afternoon*
dziękuję za (dziękować > podziękować) *thank you for*
dziennikarz (m) / dziennikarka (f) *journalist*
dziś *today*

emerytką (emerytka) *retired woman*

fantastyczną wiadomość (fantastyczny, wiadomość) *a fantastic piece of news*
fascynującą informację (fascynujący, informacja) *a fascinating piece of information*
fotografie (fotografia) *photographs*
Francuz *French (man)*
Francuzka *French (woman)*

galerie (galeria) *gallery*
gdzie *where*
genealogiem (genealog) *genealogist*
głodny *hungry*
gościem (gość) *guest*
gronostaj *ermine*

herbatę (herbata) *tea*
herbaty (herbata) *some tea*
hotelu (hotel) *hotel*

i *and*
imię *first name*
interesującą wiadomość (interesujący, wiadomość) *an interesting piece of news*
Irlandka *Irish (woman)*
Irlandczyk *Irish (man)*
iść *to go*

jak daleko (jak, daleko) *how far away?*
jaką (jaki) *what, what sort of?*
jaki *what kind of?, what a*
jakichś krewnych (jakiś krewny) *any relatives*
Japończyk *Japanese (man)*
Japonka *Japanese (woman)*
jest (być) *he/she/it is*
jestem *I'm*
jesteśmy umówieni (umówiony; umawiać się > umówić się) *we've got an appointment, we've arranged a meeting*
jeszcze *still, besides, more, yet*
jutro *tomorrow*
już *already, now*

Kanadyjka *Canadian (woman)*
Kanadyjczyk *Canadian (man)*
kartą kredytową (karta kredytowa) *by credit card*
kiedyś *ever, at any time, one day*
kilka *a few, several*
kim (kto) *what (in terms of profession)*
kim pani była (kto, pani, być) *what/who were you?, what did you do?*
kompletnie (kompletny) *completely*
koniecznie *necessarily, absolutely (must)*
kontakty (kontakt) *contacts*
korytarzem (korytarz) *along the corridor*
książki (książka) *books*
Kto? *Who?*
Kto to jest? *Who is it (this)?*
Która godzina? (który, godzina) *What's the time (which hour?)*

kuchnia *kitchen, cuisine, food*
kuchnię (kuchnia) *kitchen, cuisine*
kupić (kupować > kupić) *buy*

lekarzem (lekarz) *doctor*
lody kawowe (lód, lody, kawowy) *coffee ice cream*
lotniczy *airmail*
ładna (ładny) *pretty*
łasiczka *(little) weasel*

ma (mieć) *(s/he/it) has*
magnesy (magnes) *(fridge) magnets*
Mam alergię na *I'm allergic to*
mama *mum*
mapa *map*
mądry (m) / mądra (f) *clever*
medycynę (medycyna) *medicine*
menadżer (m) / menadżerka (f) *manager*
męża (mąż) *husband*
mieszkali (mieszkać) *lived*
mogę (móc) *I can, I may*
moi przodkowie (mój, przodek) *my ancestors*
moja (mój) *my (f.)*
można *it's possible to*
mój *my (used with masc. nouns)*
mówi (mówić > powiedzieć) *is speaking, speaks*
musi pan *you must, sir*
muszę (musieć) *I must/I have to*
Muszę już iść. *I must go now./I have to go now.*
muzea (muzeum) *museums*

na + loc. *(located) on, at*
na emeryturze (na, emerytura) *on a pension, retired*
na którą godzinę (która godzina) *what time for? when for*
na parterze (parter) *on the ground floor*
na prawo od *on/to the right of*
naprawdę *really*
narodowe (narodowy) *national*
nauczyciel (m) / nauczycielka (f) *teacher*
nazwiska (nazwisko) *surname*
nie *no, not*
nie ma za co *not at all, no problem, don't mention it, it's OK*
nie wiem (wiedzieć) *I don't know.*
niedaleko + gen. *not far away (from)*
niedaleko Krakowa *near, not far from Kraków*
Niemiec *German (man)*
Niemka *German (woman)*
niestety *unfortunately, sadly*
Nigeryjka *Nigerian (woman)*
Nigeryjczyk *Nigerian (man)*
no *well, then, yes*
nonsens *rubbish, nonsense*

o czwartej *at four*
o której *at what time*
obejrzeć (oglądać > obejrzeć) *(have a) look at*
obiad *lunch, dinner*
obok Rynku *next to the Market Square*
obrazy (obraz) *paintings*
oczywiście (oczywisty) *certainly, obviously*
od domu (dom) *from the house*
od Krakowa *from Kraków*
ojciec *father*

pani (to a woman) *Madam/Mrs/Ms, lady*
pani mąż *your husband, madam*
panu (pan) *Sir/Mr, gentleman*
park *park*
partner (m) / partnerka (f) *partner*
pewnie (pewny) *certainly, surely*
pieniądze (pl.) *money*
pies *dog*

piwo *beer/lager*
plakaty (plakat) *posters*
po + loc. *after, along, by*
po drodze (po, droga) *on the way*
po południu *in the afternoon, this afternoon*
po schodach (schody) *by the stairs, along the stairs*
pochodzą z + gen. (pochodzić) *come, originate from*
pocztówki (pocztówka) *postcard*
podjazdem (dla osób niepełnosprawnych) (podjazd) *down/up the ramp (for wheelchair users)*
pojechać (jechać > pojechać) *go (other than on foot)*
pojechać drogą na + acc. *take the road to*
Polką (Polka) *Polish woman*
poproszę (prosić > poprosić) *please (extra polite), I'll ask for*
portret *portrait*
potem *then, next, afterwards*
potrzebuję pomocy (potrzebować + gen., pomoc) *I need help*
poza tym (poza, to) *besides (that)*
pracuje (pracować > popracować) *she works*
prawie *almost*
prawnik *lawyer*
priorytet *priority*
problem *problem*
programista (m) / programistka (f) *programmer*
prosto (prosty) *straight (on)*
proszę (prosić > poprosić) *please*
prowadzi do (prowadzić > poprowadzić) *leads, takes you to*
prywatnym (prywatny) *private*
przejść (przechodzić > przejść) *go/come through, go/come across*
przepraszam (przepraszać > przeprosić) *sorry, excuse me, I apologize.*
przeszłość *the past*
przewodnik *guide(book)*
przy figurce (przy, figurka) *by a small statue*
przyjaciółka *(female) friend*
przyjaźni (przyjaźń) *of friendship*
przykro mi (przykry, ja) *I'm sorry.*
przyrodnia siostra *step-sister*
przyrodni brat *step-brother*
pytać o + acc. (pytać > zapytać) *ask about*

rachunek *check*
recepcja *reception (desk)*
restauracja (f.) *restaurant*
robić zdjęcia (robić > zrobić; zdjęcie) *take photographs*
rodzina; rodziny *family*
rodzinne (rodzinny) *family (adjective)*
rozpakować się (rozpakowywać się > rozpakować się) *get unpacked*
rozumiem (rozumieć > zrozumieć) *I understand, I gather*
rozwiedziony (m) / rozwiedziona (f) *divorced (singular)*
rozwiedzeni *divorced (plural)*
rynek *market , market square*

sernik *cheesecake*
skrecić w prawo (skręcać > skręcić) *turn right*
słucham (słuchać) *hello, I'm listening, Pardon?, Can I help you?*
Słucham państwa. *Can I help you? (lit: I'm listening, ladies and gentlemen)*
słychać + acc. *. . . can be heard*
słynny *famous*
smutny (m) / smutna (f) *sad*
spotkać się (spotykać się > spotkać się) *meet, get together*

spotkanie *meeting, get-together*
spraw (sprawa) *thing, matter, problem*
stary dom *an old house*
stąd *from here*
stolik (m.) *table in a restaurant, small table*
studentką (studentka) *female student*
studiuje (studiować) *s/he studies, is a student of*
Sukiennice (pl.) *the Cloth Hall*
szczęśliwy (m) / szczęśliwa (f) *happy*
syna (syna) *son*
szkockie korzenie (szkocki, korzeń) *Scottish roots*
szkoda *pity, shame, damage, waste*
szkoda, że *it's a pity (that)*
Szkotem (Szkot) *Scot(sman)*
szuka + gen. (szukać > poszukać) *is looking for*
szuka pan rodziny (szukać > *poszukać, rodzina) you're looking for relatives*

ta droga *that road, the path*
tak *yes*
także *also*
też *too, also, as well*
to jest (być) *this is, it's*
To żaden problem. *It's no problem at all.*
trochę *a little bit*
trzeba *one needs to*
tuż obok + gen. *right next door (to)*
usiąść (siadać > usiąść) *to sit down*

w + acc. *into, to*
w + locative *in*
w dół *downwards*
w lewo *left/on the left*
w Polsce (Polska) *in Poland*
w sklepie muzealnym (sklep, muzealny) *in the museum shop*
w twoim hotelu (twój hotel) *at/in your hotel*
warto *worth*
wczoraj *yesterday*
weganinem (weganin) *vegan (m)*
weganką (weganka) *vegan (f)*
wegetarianinem (wegetarianin) *vegetarian (m)*
wegetarianką (wegetarianka) *vegetarian (f)*
wejść *come in/go in*
widać + acc. *can be seen*
widokówka *postcard*
wiedziałem (wiedzieć) *I knew (said by a man)*
więc *so*
windą (winda) *in the lift*
wolno *it's allowed, one may*
wrócić do + gen. (wracać > wrócić) *come/go back to*
wsi (wieś) *of a village*
wszystko *everything, all*
wygląda, że (wyglądać) *it looks as if*
wyjść (wychodzić > wyjść) *go out, come out*
wykluczone (wykluczony; wykluczać > wykluczyć) *excluded, out of the question*
wymienić (wymieniać > wymienić) *change, exchange, enumerate*
wypadek *accident*
wytłumaczę ci (tłumaczyć > wytłumaczyć, ty) *I'll explain to you*

z + instr. *with*
z Ewą (Ewa) *with Ewa*
z muzeum + gen. *from/out of the museum*
z tobą (ty) *with you*
za + acc. *(moving) behind*
za + instr. *(located) behind*
zadzwonić (dzwonić > zadzwonić) *ring, phone*
zakładki (zakładka) *bookmarks*

załatwić (załatwiać > załatwić) *deal with, do, settle*
zamówić (zamawiać > zamówić) *to order*
zapłacić (płacić > zapłacić) *pay*
zapłacić za + acc. (płacić > zapłacić) *pay for*
zapytać (pytać > zapytać) *ask*
zasięgnąć informacji (zasięgać > zasięgnąć, informacje (pl.)) *get some information*
zawrócić (zawracać > zawrócić) *turn round, turn back*
zły *bad, angry (about a dog: aggressive)*
zmęczony (męczyć > zmęczyć) *tired*
znaczek *stamp*
znaczki (znaczek) *stamps*
znaleźć (znajdować > znaleźć) *find*
znowu *again*
zobaczyć (widzieć > zobaczyć) *see*
zwiedzić (zwiedzać > zwiedzić) *visit, go sightseeing in*
zwykły *ordinary, usual*
żaden *none*
żona *wife*

Grammar appendix

ADJECTIVES

Adjectives are natural companions to nouns as they help describe nouns:

angielski detektyw	*English detective*
interesująca wiadomość	*interesting news*

Adjectives have three genders and usually agree with the gender of the noun:

angielski detektyw (masculine)	*English detective*
angielska książka (feminine)	*English book*
angielskie piwo (neuter)	*English beer*

Adjectives usually precede nouns (**nowy samochód** – *a new car*) but may follow to clarify the meaning of a multiple-meaning noun:

straż pożarna	*fire service*	**straż miejska**	*municipal guard*

ADVERBS

Adverbs are companions to verbs and are often derived from adjectives:

Adjective	Adverb
zimne piwo (*cold beer*)	**Jest zimno.** (*It's cold.*)
piękna pogoda (*lovely weather*)	**Jest pięknie.** (*It's lovely.*)
prosta droga (*straight road*)	**iść prosto** (*to go straight ahead*)

ADVERBIALS

Adverbials provide additional information by answering questions such as:

Kiedy?	*When?*
dzisiaj	*today*
w piątek	*on Friday*
Gdzie?	*Where?*
daleko	*far away*
na Rynku	*in the Market Square*
Jak?	*How?*

spokojnie	*calmly*
prosto	*straight ahead*
Dlaczego?	*Why?*
żeby odpoczął	*so he could rest*
Ile?	*How much/many?*
dużo	*a lot*
mało	*a little*

Please note that not all adverbials are adverbs. For example:

w piątek	*on Friday*
na Rynku	*in the Market Square*

ARTICLES: DEFINITE AND INDEFINITE (*A, AN, THE*)

Polish doesn't have definite or indefinite articles. Context can tell you to if a noun is definite or indefinite. **Kobieta** can be *a woman* as well as *the woman.*

CASE

Nominative (who?/what?) *Mianownik (kto?/co?)*

- plays the role of a subject in a sentence

To jest detektyw.	*This is a detective.*

Genitive (of who?/of what?) *Dopełniacz (kogo?/czego?)*

- expresses possession (when English uses 's or *of*)
- expresses absence or lack

Nie ma czasu.	*There's no time.*

- is used with expressions of quantity

szklanka wody	*a glass of water*

- is used after the number five and upwards

pięć domów	*five houses*

- is used with some prepositions

od	*from*	**daleko od domu**	*far from home*
do	*to*	**do domu**	*(to) home*
dla	*for*	**dla mamy**	*for Mum*
naprzeciw (ko)	*opposite*	**naprzeciwko domu**	*opposite the house*
obok	*next to*	**obok domu**	*next to the house*

blisko	*near*	**blisko domu**	*near the house*
niedaleko	*not far from*	**niedaleko domu**	*not far from the house*
u	*at*	**u przyjaciół**	*at friends'*
wokół	*around*	**wokół domu**	*around the house*
z/ze	*from*	**z Londynu**	*from London*

Dative (to whom?/to what?) *Celownik (komu?/czemu?)*

▶ expresses an indirect object

Andrew daje Marii swojego maila. *Andrew gives his email address to Maria.*

▶ is used in certain impersonal expressions

Bardzo mi miło. *Pleased to meet you.*

Wszystkim jest trudno. *We all find it difficult.*

Accusative (whom?/what?) *Biernik (kogo?/co?)*

▶ expresses the direct object

▶ is used after **mieć** (*to have*)

Mam samochód. *I've got a car.*

▶ is used with prepositions related to verbs of motion

Idę na spacer. *I'm going for a walk.*

▶ is used with days of the week

w sobotę *on Saturday*

▶ is used when referring to playing games

grać w tenisa *play tennis*

Instrumental ((with) whom?/(with) what?) *Narzędnik ((z) kim?/(z) czym?)*

▶ is used after **być** (*to be*) to express nationality, profession or identity

Jestem Anglikiem. *I'm English.*

Toffik jest dobrym psem. *Toffik is a good dog.*

▶ is used with expressions of time

wieczorem *in the evening*

nocą *at night*

▶ is used to express means by which an action is performed

Jadę autobusem. *I'm going by bus.*

Płacę kartą zbliżeniową. *I'm paying with a contactless card.*

Locative (about whom?/about what?/where?) *Miejscownik (o kim?/o czym?/gdzie?)*

▶ indicates time and place of action after the following prepositions

na	**na przystanku**	*at the bus stop*
po	**po obiedzie**	*after dinner*
przy	**przy hotelu**	*by the hotel*
w	**w styczniu**	*in January*

Nouns in the locative case are always preceded by a preposition.

Vocative *Wołacz* **– the attention getting case**

▶ is used to address whoever we are speaking or writing to directly

Haniu! **Kasiu!** **Mario!** **Panie Olku!** **Amelko!**

Ty idioto! *You idiot!*

NOUNS

A noun is a word which names or refers to:

- ▶ a person (**mężczyzna,** *a man*, **kobieta,** *a woman*, **dziecko**, *a child*)
- ▶ an object (**stół**, *a table*; **książka**, *a book*; **samochód**, *a car*)
- ▶ an animal or a plant (**pies**, *a dog*; **kot**, *a cat*; **tulipan**, *a tulip*)
- ▶ an abstract concept (**chwila**, *a moment*)
- ▶ a place (**Anglia**, *England*; **Polska**, *Poland*)
- ▶ a natural phenomenon (**mgła**, *fog*; **deszcz**, *rain*)

There are two important things to know about nouns:

1 They have a gender whether they are animate or inanimate.

Masculine: detektyw (*a detective*) **stół** (*a table*) **pies** (*a dog*)

Typically, masculine nouns end in a consonant (e.g. **-b**, **-k**, **-l**, **-w**, **-m**). Some exceptions: **dentysta** (*a dentist*), **kierowca** (*a driver*) and **mężczyzna** (*a man*).

Feminine: kobieta (*a woman*) **książka** (a book) **ulica** (*a street*)

Most feminine nouns end in **-a**.

Neuter: nazwisko (*surname*) **mleko** (*milk*) **dziecko** (*child*)

Typically, neuter nouns end in **-o** or **-e**.

2 Nouns have different forms for expressing grammatical cases (seven in total) related to the function they play in the sentence.

Neuter nouns

Case	Singular	Plural
Nominative	**nazwisko**	**nazwiska**
Genitive	**nazwiska**	**nazwisk**
Dative	**nazwisku**	**nazwiskom**
Accusative	**nazwisko**	**nazwiska**
Instrumental	**nazwiskiem**	**nazwiskami**
Locative	**nazwisku**	**nazwiskach**
Vocative	**nazwisko!**	**nazwiska!**

PRONOUNS

Pronouns refer to things without naming them.

Personal pronoun	Possessive pronoun – masculine	Possessive pronoun – feminine	Possessive pronoun – neuter
ja (*I*)	**mój** (*my*)	**moja**	**moje**
ty (*you*)	**twój** (*your*)	**twoja**	**twoje**
on (*he*)	**jego** (*his*)	**jego**	**jego**
ona (*she*)	**jej** (*her*)	**jej**	**jej**
ono (*it*)	**jego** (*its*)	**jego**	**jego**
my (*we*)	**nasz** (*our*)	**nasza**	**nasze**
wy (*you*)	**wasz** (*your*)	**wasza**	**wasze**
oni/one (*they*)	**ich** (*their*)	**ich**	**ich**

Declination of singular masculine possessive pronoun, adjective and noun:

Nominative	**mój**	**angielski**	**detektyw**
Genitive	**mojego**	**angielskiego**	**detektywa**
Dative	**mojemu**	**angielskiemu**	**detektywowi**
Accusative	**mojego**	**angielskiego**	**detektywa**
Instrumental	**moim**	**angielskim**	**detektywem**
Locative	**moim**	**angielskim**	**detektywie**
Vocative	**o mój**	**angielski**	**detektywie!**

Declination of singular feminine possessive pronoun, adjective and noun:

Nominative	**moja**	**angielska**	**książka**
Genitive	**mojej**	**angielskiej**	**książki**
Dative	**mojej**	**angielskiej**	**książce**
Accusative	**moją**	**angielską**	**książkę**
Instrumental	**moją**	**angielską**	**książką**
Locative	**mojej**	**angielskiej**	**książce**
Vocative	**o moja**	**angielska**	**książko!**

Declination of singular neuter possessive pronoun, adjective and noun:

Nominative	**moje**	**angielskie**	**piwo**
Genitive	**mojego**	**angielskiego**	**piwa**
Dative	**mojemu**	**angielskiemu**	**piwu**
Accusative	**moje**	**angielskie**	**piwo**
Instrumental	**moim**	**angielskim**	**piwem**
Locative	**moim**	**angielskim**	**piwie**
Vocative	**o moje**	**angielskie**	**piwo!**

NUMBERS

Numbers in Polish align themselves to nouns, matching their gender. There are cardinal numbers ('how many' / show quantity – one, two, three) and ordinal numbers (order – first, second, third).

SENTENCE PATTERNS

▶ **To + być** (to be) + noun (nominative)

To + **jest** + **detektyw.** (nominative)

This + is + a detective.

To + **są** + **słynne obrazy**. (adjective + noun nom.)

These + are + famous paintings.

▶ **Subject + być** (*to be*) + noun (instrumental)

Anastazja (subject) + **jest** + **Ukrainką.** (noun instrumental)

Anastazja + is + Ukrainian.

Baljit (subject) + **jest** + **studentem.** (noun instrumental)

Baljit + is + a student.

▶ **Subject + mieć** (*to have*) + noun (accusative)

Ja (subject) + **mam** + **dokument.** (noun accusative)

I + have + a document.

Tosia (subject) + **ma** + **rodzinę.** (noun accusative)

Tosia + has + a family.

Andrew (subject) + **ma** + **rodzinne dokumenty.** (adjective + noun accusative)

Andrew + has + family documents.

▶ **Subject + nie mieć** (*to have not*) + noun (genitive)

Ja (subject) + **nie mam** + **dokumentu.** (genitive)

I + haven't got + a document.

Andrew (subject) + **nie ma** + **czasu.** (genitive)

Andrew + hasn't got + time.

▶ **Poproszę** + noun (accusative)

Poproszę + **sok.** (noun accusative)

Can I have + juice?

Poproszę + **mapę.** (noun accusative)

Can I have + a map?

▶ **Subject + musieć** (*must*) + verb (infinitive) + rest of the sentence (RS)

If the rest of the sentence is a noun, it will be in the accusative.

Leila (subject) + **musi** + **zwiedzić** (verb – infinitive) + **Kraków.** (RS/acc)

Leila + must + visit + Kraków.

Nguyen (subject) + **musi** + **wymienić** (verb – infinitive) + **pieniądze.** (RS/acc)

Nguyen + must + exchange + money.

▶ **Subject + nie musieć** (*do not have to*) + verb (infinitive) + RS

If RS is a noun then it will be in the genitive.

Leila (subject) + **nie musi** + **zwiedzić** (verb – infinitive) + **Krakowa.**

Leila + doesn't have to + visit + Kraków.

Nguyen (subject) + **nie musi** + **wymienić** (verb – infinitive) + **pieniędzy.**

Nguyen + doesn't have to + exchange + money.

Note: **Chciał(a)by** follows the same pattern as **musieć** (above).

▶ **Subject + lubić** (*to like*) + noun (accusative)

Nikola (subject) + **lubi** + **czekoladę.** (noun acc.)

Nikola + likes + chocolate.

▶ **Subject + nie lubić** (*do not like*) + noun (genitive)

Nikola (subject) + **nie lubi** + **czekolady.** (noun gen.)

Nikola + doesn't like + chocolate.

▶ **Subject + lubić** (*to like*) + verb (infinitive/imperfective) + RS

Andrew (subject) + **lubi** + **zwiedzać** (verb) + **Kraków.** (RS/Acc.)

Andrew + likes + visiting + Kraków.

▶ **Subject + nie lubić** (*do not like*) + verb (infinitive/imperfective) + RS

Andrew (subject) + **nie lubi** + **zwiedzać** (verb) + **Krakowa.** (RS/gen.)

Andrew + doesn't like + visiting + Kraków.

'2–4 AND 5+' RULE

In Polish when you talk about two, three or four things, you use basic nominative plural forms, but when you talk about five or more (up to 21) things you use the genitive plural forms. The numbers 22, 23 and 24 follow the same pattern as two, three and four, and so on.

2	**dwa obrazy**	*two paintings*
3	**trzy obrazy**	
4	**cztery obrazy**	
5–21	**pięć obrazów–dwadzieścia jeden obrazów**	
22	**dwadzieścia dwa obrazy**	
23	**dwadzieścia trzy obrazy**	
24	**dwadzieścia cztery obrazy**	

VERBS

Verbs are words that refer to action (to go, to sit, to write, to speak, to love, to hate, etc.). Verbs have forms for different tenses (past, present or future).

pojechać	*to go*
pojechałem	*I went*

pojadę	*I will go*

Verbs have different forms for different 'persons' (I, you, he, she, etc.):

ja jadę	*I go*	**my jedziemy**	*we go*
ty jedziesz	*you (singular) go*	**wy jedziecie**	*you (plural) go*
on jedzie	*he goes*	**oni/one jadą**	*they go*
ona jedzie	*she goes*		
ono jedzie	*it goes*		

There are also other forms, such as the infinitive (dictionary) form:

czytać	*to read*
pisać	*to write*
jeść	*to eat*

'Aspect' is how a verb presents an action or situation: not summed up (imperfective) or summed up (perfective). Imperfective verbs have a present tense, as well as a future and a past. Perfective verbs in Polish have no present tense for referring to present time but have a simple future.

Czytam książkę.	*I'm reading a book.*	(present)
Czytałem książkę.	*I was reading a book.*	(past)
Będę cztać książkę.	*I will be reading a book.*	(future)
Przeczytałem książkę.	*I read a book.*	(past)
Przeczytam książkę.	*I will read a book.*	(future)

Reflexive verbs describe action happening to ourselves or to a group of specific people and are indicated by the presence of **się**.

obawiam się	*I'm afraid*
myję się	*I'm washing myself*
spotkamy się	*we will meet*

Się is never stressed and tends to blend with the verb that precedes it.

Conversation translations

01.02

Andrew	Good morning, madam. I'm Andrew Stewart.
Maria	Good morning, sir. I'm Maria Grajewska.
Andrew	Pleased to meet you.
Maria	Come in, please. Take a seat, please. Are you tired?
Andrew	Yes, a little bit.
Maria	And are you hungry?
Andrew	No. I'm not hungry.

01.04

Maria	Are you Scottish or English?
Andrew	I'm half Scottish and half English. And you? Are you Polish?
Maria	Yes, I'm Polish, but I have Scottish roots.
Andrew	What do you do?
Maria	I'm retired. And you?
Andrew	I'm a private detective.
Maria	Really?

02.02

Maria	This is my dog, Azor.
Andrew	Is it a bad dog?
Maria	No! Azor is a very good dog.

02.03

Andrew	This is my family. My wife, Jenny.
Maria	She's very pretty.
Andrew	And this is my daughter, Molly. She's a student.
Maria	What does she study?
Andrew	Medicine.
Maria	And who's this?
Andrew	This is my father, Thomas.

02.05

Andrew	Who is this?
Maria	This is my grandfather, Tomasz.
Andrew	And this?
Maria	This is my mum, Teresa.
Andrew	And this? Who is this?
Maria	This is my father, Jakub.

03.02

Maria	Do you have any family in Poland?
Andrew	I think so, but I've got a problem.
Maria	What kind of problem?
Andrew	I haven't got a name or an address.
Maria	That's not a problem. I've got contacts at the archives. Have you still got time for tea?
Andrew	Yes, I've got lots of time.
Maria	Have you got any family documents?
Andrew	Yes, I have. Here you are. These are documents and photographs.
Maria	Thank you.

03.05

Andrew	Do you have any family?
Maria	Yes, I do. I have a husband and a son. This is my son. He is an architect. He has a good job and money, but he doesn't have children.
Andrew	And your husband?
Maria	My husband's name is Piotr. He's also retired.

04.02

Andrew	Excuse me, what time is it?
Maria	It's 4 o'clock.
Andrew	Unfortunately, I've got to go now.
Maria	Oh, that's a pity. Why do you have to go now?
Andrew	I've got a few things to do. I have to go back to the hotel and unpack. Then I have to exchange some money and call home.
Maria	You have to visit Kraków as well.
Andrew	Oh yes, definitely.
Maria	We have to meet again.
Andrew	Yes. I'd love to.

05.02

Andrew	Thank you for meeting me.
Maria	You're welcome.
Andrew	I'd love to find my family so much.
Maria	Of course, I understand. See you tomorrow.

05.03

Receptionist	Good morning, reception. How can I help?
Andrew	Good morning. I'd like to book a table at the restaurant.
Receptionist	For what time?
Andrew	For 7:30.
Receptionist	Can I have your name please?
Andrew	Stewart.
Receptionist	Mr. Andrew Stewart?
Andrew	Yes.
Receptionist	Room number 125?
Andrew	Yes.
Receptionist	That's all sorted.
Andrew	Thank you very much. Good bye.

05.04

Ewa	Hello?
Maria	Hi. It's Maria.
Ewa	Hi. How are you?
Maria	I'm good, thank you. I'd like to meet you. I need help.
Ewa	What kind of help?
Maria	I need some advice and I need to find some documents.
Ewa	OK.

06.02

Waitress	Good morning. How can I help you?
Maria	Can I have coffee and a cheesecake, please?
Andrew	And can I have some tea and coffee ice cream, please?
Waitress	No problem.

06.03

Maria	Can I have the check, please?
Waitress	Here you are.
Andrew	I'd like to pay the check.
Maria	No way. You're my guest.
Andrew	Thank you so much.

06.05

Andrew	Can I have this postcard, please?
Woman	Here you are.
Andrew	How much is it?
Woman	Two fifty.

06.06

Sales assistant	How can I help?
Andrew	Can I have a stamp for Great Britain, please?
Sales assistant	Regular or first class?
Andrew	First class, please.

07.02

Andrew	I'm a little bit hungry.
Maria	Let's go for dinner. Do you like Polish cuisine?
Andrew	Yes, I like hunter's stew, cheesecake and Polish beer.

07.03

Maria	What would you like to see in Kraków?
Andrew	I'd like to see the Market Square, the Cloth Hall, Wawel and the National Museum.

07.06

Maria	Do you like Leonardo da Vinci's paintings?
Andrew	Yes, I like them a lot. Why do you ask?
Maria	There's a famous painting by Leonardo in Krakow - *Lady with an Ermine*. Would you like to see it?
Andrew	I'd love to. I like visiting galleries and museums.

08.02

Andrew	Is taking photos allowed in the museum?
Maria	No, it's not allowed. I'm sorry.
Andrew	That's a pity. Where can you buy a guidebook?
Maria	In the museum shop.
Andrew	What else can you buy there?
Maria	Books, coffee table books, posters, bookmarks, fridge magnets, postcards, etc.
Andrew	And can you buy stamps?
Maria	I don't know. You have to ask.

08.04

Andrew	Where is the shop? Do you have to leave the museum?
Maria	No, you can go down the corridor to get to the shop. You need to go straight on, then down the stairs. The shop is on the ground floor.
Andrew	What else is worth buying from the shop?

08.05

Andrew	Excuse me. Can I pay by credit card?
Sales assistant	Yes, you can.

09.02

Andrew	Hello?
Maria	Good morning Andrzeju (vocative form of Andrzej—the Polish version of Andrew—used in direct address). It's Maria.
Andrew	Good morning Mario (vocative form of Maria used in direct address). How are you?
Maria	I'm well, thank you. I've got an interesting piece of information for you. When can we meet?
Andrew	Today?
Maria	Fine.
Andrew	Where?
Maria	At your hotel.
Andrew	What time?
Maria	At 4 o'clock.
Andrew	OK. See you.
Maria	Good bye.

09.03

Andrew	What happened?
Maria	I've got a fascinating piece of information for you.
Andrew	What kind of information?
Maria	Let's go. I'll explain everything on the way.
Andrew	Where are we going?
Maria	Not far. To Sienna Street. Right by the Market Square. We've got an appointment with Ewa.

09.05

Andrew	Who is Ewa?
Maria	Ewa is a friend of mine. She works at the Archive. She's a genealogist.

09.06

Maria	Ewo (vocative form of Ewa used in direct address) – this is Mr. Andrew Stewart.
Ewa	Good morning, sir.
Andrew	Pleased to meet you.
Ewa	Let's go into my office.
Ewa	I understand you're looking for family in Poland.
Andrew	Yes. I know that my ancestors come from Poland.
Ewa	Your ancestors lived in Poland, but they were Scottish. The family home – an old manor house – is in Nowe Szkoty.

10.02

Andrew	How far is Nowe Szkoty?
Maria	Not far – 20 kilometers to the west of Kraków.
Andrew	Have you ever been there?
Maria	Yes, many years ago.

10.03

Maria	Excuse me, what happened?
Police officer	An accident. The road is closed. Where are you going?
Maria	To Nowe Szkoty.
Police officer	You need to turn back then, and take the road towards Tarnów.
Maria	OK. Thank you.

10.05

Maria	Excuse me, madam. How can I get to the old manor house?
Woman	You need to go straight on, up to the church. Turn right by the church and go up to a small crossroads by a statue. From there, turn left. That road leads up to the old manor house.
Maria	Straight on, up to the church, right, then left by the statue.
Woman	Yes.
Maria	OK. Thank you very much, madam.
Woman	You're welcome.

Can-do statements

UNIT	CEFR level	ACTFL level	CAN-DO STATEMENTS
UNIT 1	**A1**	**Novice High**	I can make an introduction by asking and answering questions about personal details such as someone's name, occupation and nationality. I can exchange and understand basic greeting and leave taking expressions.
UNIT 2	**A1 / A2**	**Novice High / Intermediate Low**	(A2) I can understand sentences and frequently used expressions describing relatives by name, age and occupation. (A1) I can deal with numbers to count family members and state people's ages.
UNIT 3	**A1 / A2**	**Novice High / Intermediate Low**	(A1) I can understand and use basic phrases to describe the date, time and today's weather. (A2) I can deal with numbers using various counters such as years of age, hours and minutes.
UNIT 4	**A1**	**Novice High**	I can understand and use simple sentences to ask for items in a shop. I can handle numbers to state prices and quantities.
UNIT 5	**A1 / A2**	**Novice High / Intermediate Low**	(A2) I can understand and use common expressions for ordering and dining in a restaurant. (A1) I can use basic phrases to describe and comment on a meal.
UNIT 6	**A1 / A2**	**Novice High / Intermediate Low**	(A1) I can recognize and use basic phrases describing a location in relation to its surroundings. (A2) I can ask for and give directions to a point of interest using frequently used expressions.

UNIT	CEFR level	ACTFL level	CAN-DO STATEMENTS
UNIT 7	A1 / A2	Novice High / Intermediate Low	(A2) I can understand and give instructions for traveling via various modes of transport to reach a destination. (A1) I can recognize and use basic phrases to compare different routes and state the time it takes.
UNIT 8	A1	Novice High	I can recognize and use basic phrases to list hobbies, likes and dislikes. I can understand simple expressions to describe the frequency one does a hobby or sport.
UNIT 9	A1	Novice High	I can form simple sentences in past tense to describe activities done in the past. I can recognize and understand basic expressions to describe a day in the past.
UNIT 10	A1	Novice High	I can form simple sentences using the future tense to describe activities that will be done in the future. I can recognize and understand basic expressions to make an appointment to meet in the future.

Notes